Patricia MacLachlan

Twayne's United States Authors Series

Ruth K. MacDonald, Editor

TUSAS 685

PATRICIA MacLACHLAN
Judy B. Messer

Twayne's United States Authors Series No. 685

Patricia MacLachlan
David L. Russell

Copyright © 1997 by Twayne Publishers

Twayne Publishers
An Imprint of Simon & Schuster Macmillan
1633 Broadway
New York, NY 10019

Library of Congress Cataloging-in-Publication Data

Russell, David L., 1946–
    Patricia MacLachlan / David L. Russell.
        p. cm. — (Twayne's United States authors series ; TUSAS 685)
    Includes bibliographical references and index.
    ISBN 0-8057-4575-0 (alk. paper)
    1. MacLachlan, Patricia—Criticism and interpretation.
2.   Children's stories, American—History and criticism.   I. Title.
II. Series.
PS3563.A3178Z86 1997
813'.54—dc21   97-7224
                                                                                                  CIP

The paper used in this publication meets the minimum requirements of American National Standard for Information Sciences—Permanence of Paper for Printed Library Materials. ANSI Z39.48-1984. ∞ ™

10 9 8 7 6 5 4 3 2 1

Printed in the United States of America

Patricia MacLachlan

David L. Russell

Ferris State University

Twayne Publishers
An Imprint of Simon & Schuster Macmillan
New York

Prentice Hall International
London • Mexico City • New Delhi • Singapore • Sydney • Toronto

To Patti, with love

Contents

Preface

A critical biography of Patricia MacLachlan may seem premature. After all, she is, at this writing, in her 50s and has been publishing books for little more than 15 years. She is by no means a prolific writer, with just eight brief novels, seven picture books, and two short-story collections to her credit. One might logically wonder if there is enough to say about her to fill a volume.

I trust when readers have finished this book they will agree that, indeed, there is a great deal that is important to say about Patricia MacLachlan. For one coming, as she did, to her profession relatively late in life, MacLachlan has accumulated an impressive publishing record. Virtually every novel she has written has won some award or recognition. She has received Golden Kite awards, ALA Notable Book citations, the Scott O'Dell Historical Fiction Award, the Newbery Medal, and the University of Southern Mississippi Medallion for the body of her work. Her novels, from the very beginning, have exhibited an extraordinary consistency in quality. She is one of the finest stylists writing for children today. Lean and lucid, her writings reflect the influence of E. B. White. And, like White's, her books are deceptively simple. The beauty of her language and the striking quality of her images linger in our memory long after we have laid aside her books. But there is more to MacLachlan's work than polished style. Perhaps what affects us most profoundly in her writings is her fundamental belief in humanity—her affirmation of the cycle of life, her understanding of the interdependence of all people, her conviction in the essential worth of humankind.

MacLachlan's achievement to date is that of a writer who has discovered her specific strengths and has exercised them fully. She is a master of the short novel and of the lyrical picture book. Her forte is realistic fiction—either historical or contemporary. Plots are less important to her than her characters. She knows the significance of the seemingly insignificant; she feels the grasshopper's burden and notes the fall of the sparrow. She has a keen insight into the mind of the preadolescent child, and she understands very clearly the give and take of successful human relationships, the many sacrifices, losses, and gains that make up living. Her stories are largely serious, tempered with a gentle humor. If we seek thrills, sensation, or the grandiose sweep of things, we will not look to MacLachlan. But if it be thoughtful provocation, sensitive insight, and the magic of language that we seek, she will not disappoint us.

Very little in the way of critical study has been done on MacLachlan, a fact that has made this project both challenging and rewarding. For interpretations, I have relied on my own reading and judgment, accompanied by what scant support I could locate in the reviews and the small handful of articles available.

Happily, I was assisted by a host of very kind people acquainted with MacLachlan and her work. First, I want to thank Bill Morris of HarperCollins Publishers, without whose assistance I fear this study would never have gotten off the ground. Not only was his help invaluable but it was given with great kindness and generosity. I received indispensable insights from MacLachlan's editors, all of whom were most accommodating. Charlotte Zolotow, herself an almost legendary figure in the world of children's literature, was MacLachlan's first editor at Harper and worked with her for many years. Ms. Zolotow was both gracious and forthright in our discussion of MacLachlan. Joanna Cotler, MacLachlan's current editor at HarperCollins, was equally kind in sharing her time. Craig Virden, who was MacLachlan's first agent and is now her editor at Delacorte as well as a close friend, also generously provided his insights.

Most of all, I wish to thank Patricia MacLachlan herself, who has been nothing but delightful in her dealings with me. She has tolerated my frequent (and, I am sure, often inconvenient) telephone calls, has provided me with written materials, but most of all has allowed me a glimpse into her life that I might better understand her writings. I hope this volume will do some justice to her literary achievement.

I leave to the last the one who has had to put up with the most, my own Patti. This is for her.

Chronology

1938   Born in Cheyenne, Wyoming, on 3 March, daughter of Philo and Madonna Moss Pritzkau (both teachers).

1944   Family moves to Rochester, Minnesota, where father becomes school supervisor.

1948   Family moves to Connecticut, where father becomes professor of curriculum at University of Connecticut.

1962   Marries Robert MacLachlan (a clinical psychologist) on 14 April and receives baccalaureate with a major in English education from the University of Connecticut.

1962–1963   English teacher, Bennett Junior High School, Manchester, Connecticut.

1964   Son John born.

1967   Son Jamie born.

1970   Daughter, Emily, born.

1970–1980   Board member, Children's Aid Family Service Agency.

1979   Publishes *The Sick Day* (Pantheon), illustrated by William Pene du Bois.

1980   Publishes *Through Grandpa's Eyes* (Harper & Row), illustrated by Deborah Ray; *Moon, Stars, Frogs, and Friends* (Pantheon), illustrated by Tomie de Paola; and *Arthur, for the Very First Time* (Harper & Row), winner of Golden Kite Award for Fiction and an ALA Notable Book.

1982   Publishes *Cassie Binegar* (Harper & Row); *Mama One, Mama Two* (Harper & Row), illustrated by Ruth Lercher Bornstein; and *Tomorrow's Wizard* (Harper & Row), illustrated by Kathy Jacobi.

1983 Publishes *Seven Kisses in a Row* (Harper & Row), a Junior Literary Guild selection.

1984 Publishes *Unclaimed Treasures* (Harper & Row), an ALA Notable Book and Golden Kite Award winner.

1985 Publishes *Sarah, Plain and Tall* (Harper & Row), an ALA Notable Book, Junior Literary Guild selection, and recipient of Scott O'Dell Historical Fiction Award.

1986 Awarded Newbery Medal for *Sarah, Plain and Tall*; appointed visiting lecturer, Smith College, Northampton, Massachusetts.

1988 Publishes *The Facts and Fictions of Minna Pratt* (Harper & Row), an ALA Notable Book.

1990 Writes the screenplay (with Carol Sobieski) for *Sarah, Plain and Tall,* a Hallmark Hall of Fame television production starring Glenn Close and Christopher Walken.

1991 Publishes *Three Names* (HarperCollins), illustrated by Alexander Pertzoff, and *Journey* (Delacorte); resigns position at Smith College.

1992 Writes *Skylark* (sequel to *Sarah, Plain and Tall),* the screenplay, also a Hallmark Hall of Fame television production.

1993 Publishes *Baby* (Delacorte).

1994 Publishes *All the Places to Love* (HarperCollins), illustrated by Mike Wimmer, and *Skylark* (HarperCollins).

1995 Publishes *What You Know First* (HarperCollins), illustrated by Barry Moser. Completes screenplay for *Journey,* a Hallmark Hall of Fame television production.

1996 Completes screenplay for *Baby.* Awarded the Medallion from the University of Southern Mississippi for the body of her work.

Chapter One

Patricia MacLachlan's Journey

What you know first stays with you.

—What You Know First

Eudora Welty observed that "In writing, as in life, the connections of all sorts of relationships and kinds lie in wait of discovery. . . ."[1] We will find no better expression of the essence of Patricia MacLachlan's writings, for her exquisite books portray children discovering who they are and how they fit into the world around them. Her career as a writer has been meteoric in its rise from obscurity to celebrity. Within just seven years of her first book publication she had received some of the most significant distinctions in the field of children's literature, including the ALA Notable Book designation, the Golden Kite Fiction Award, the Scott O'Dell Historical Fiction Award, and the Newbery Medal. These accolades must have been overwhelming indeed for someone who did not begin writing seriously until she was in her mid-30s and who was 40 before her first book was published. However, MacLachlan has been a constant observer of the world around her, absorbing the experiences and personalities, making the connections, and discovering the relationships. All her life, she was unwittingly preparing to become a writer.

The most personal of writers, Patricia MacLachlan writes about the people she knows, the places she has lived, and the experiences she has enjoyed or endured. More than once in her books, MacLachlan makes reference to the importance of "what you know first," those indelible memories from our childhood that will forever be a part of our lives. Even a cursory glance at MacLachlan's own early life will illustrate the enormous influence of the people and places of her childhood.

She was born Patricia Pritzkau, the only child of Philo and Madonna Moss Pritzkau, in Cheyenne, Wyoming, on 3 March

1938. The family lived in Cheyenne until Patricia was in the first grade, in 1944, when her father accepted the position of school supervisor in Rochester, Minnesota. Her early memories were happy ones; her parents were devoted to her and taught her the pleasures of reading and music and art. Her parents bought her a piano when she was four, and that was the beginning of a lifelong love affair with music. However, her piano lessons were somewhat less than successful. She recalls: "I might be a musician today except for two things. First of all, the piano had mirrors on it. Instead of practicing I began talking to the face in the mirror, creating conversations and complicated continuing plots. The second problem caused my piano teacher to throw up his hands. 'She makes up the music,' he complained. 'She changes Mozart.' "[2] Her lively imagination was certainly nurtured by her parents, who were exceedingly tolerant, and encouraged by her status as an only child who frequently had to entertain herself. She recalls hiding beneath her parents' huge dining table, skirted by a generous tablecloth that hung to the floor, and eavesdropping on adult conversations—an experience that would find its way into *Cassie Binegar*. She also invented an imaginary companion named Mary, who acquired a richly developed personality, was long a constant presence in the Pritzkau household, and was amiably accepted by MacLachlan's parents. MacLachlan even recalls inventing Mary's mother, "a freewheeling, permissive woman who, in my words, 'wanted Mary to be creative on the wall.' "[3] All this certainly seems a foreshadowing of her eventual, more serious creative pursuits. Although there were only the three of them, the household seemed lively, largely because the Pritzkaus were lively people. (MacLachlan's father, Professor Pritzkau, in his 90s at this writing, still travels over the world and lectures.)

MacLachlan's parents were both natives of the West, her father born of Russian extraction in Napoleon, North Dakota, and her mother born in Lincoln, Kansas. Her father was proud of his heritage and valued his ethnic roots (demonstrated in his preference for borscht). In much the same way, his daughter would develop deep feelings for her own beginnings and celebrate in her writings a pride of place and a regard for her childhood influences. Professor Pritzkau spent his career in education, beginning as a school-teacher then moving into administration and finally into college teaching. MacLachlan's mother began training as a teacher; however, aside from serving a brief stint as a secretary in the school system very early on and later taking a job to help pay for her daughter's college education, she did not work outside the home.

The memories of a very happy childhood have played an important role in MacLachlan's writing. In her early years, she developed her voracious reading habits—an example set by her parents—and in addition to the piano, she studied the cello, which she enjoys playing to this day. Her cello playing would be the chief inspiration for *The Facts and Fictions of Minna Pratt,* a book that is almost an homage to music for the important role it has played in MacLachlan's life. A gregarious child, she also developed very strong childhood friendships and, in fact, still maintains contact with several elementary school friends from her Connecticut days. In short, she recalls having loved childhood.

Surprisingly, the childhood memories that have played the least important role in her writing are those surrounding her formal education, perhaps because her days in school paled in comparison to her stimulating life at home. For MacLachlan, school was downright uninspiring, even stifling—a fact that may have contributed to her relatively late development as a writer. The only piece MacLachlan can remember writing in elementary school was in response to an assignment: "Write a story for tomorrow," her teacher said. "It must have a beginning, a middle and an end, and it must be about your pets." MacLachlan still possesses the three-by-five card on which she wrote her story: "My cats have names and seem happy. Often they play. The end." MacLachlan recalls that her teacher "was not impressed" and that she was discouraged from writing thereafter, which may have prompted her diary entry proclaiming, "I shall try not to be a writer."[4] Simply put, the important things in her life did not happen in school. Schools and schoolteachers play almost no role in her books, most of which are set during summer vacation. And when a teacher is portrayed, such as Miss Barbizon in *The Facts and Fictions of Minna Pratt*, the result is unflattering, to say the least. This sin of omission is all the more surprising when we consider that MacLachlan's parents were both teachers and she herself has been a teacher. Not until 1993, in *Baby*, did she portray a teacher—Ms. Minifred—in a positive role.

Like the families MacLachlan writes about, her own family was small. As mentioned previously, she was an only child, and the only grandparent she knew was her maternal grandfather. Some elderly aunts and uncles occasionally figured into the picture, but her extended family did not play a significant role in her development, a fact belied by her insightful books on intergenerational relationships. However, she did not begin her writing career in earnest until she had children of her own, and it is from her observations of their behavior and their interaction with their grandparents, her own aging parents, that MacLachlan has drawn much of her material.

In 1948, the family made its final move in its gradual eastward progress across the United States, this time to Connecticut where her father accepted a position as professor of curriculum at the University of Connecticut in Storrs. MacLachlan has lived in New England ever since, although she frequently travels to the West. Her western roots have been most vividly reflected in *Sarah, Plain and Tall* and in some of her picture books—most notably *All the Places to Love* and *What You Know First* (the latter, about a young girl whose family is leaving the West for the seacoast, is clearly autobiographical in its inspiration). However, in many of her stories there is a distinctly New England flavor, with references to lush gardens, old houses, and in some stories, the sea itself. All of her writings carry a deep sense of place, of belonging somewhere. MacLachlan believes that people write out of their landscapes, and her landscape is an amalgam of rural, independent New England and the more rugged, but equally individualistic, West. And when she writes of the city (*The Facts and Fictions of Minna Pratt* is the only significant example), it is a city with parks and trees and cheerful neighborhoods, an atmosphere almost every bit as placid as Aunt Elda's enchanting farm in *Arthur, for the Very First Time*.

MacLachlan's love of rural life stems from her childhood experiences. She spent most of her formative years living in rural areas (except for the Rochester years when the family lived in the sub-urbs). She enjoyed the rustic setting of the University of Connecti-cut, where her family first lived in group housing—converted bar-racks originally built for returning GIs after the Second World War. She happily recalls the communal atmosphere of those apart-ments, with walls so thin that her mother, while taking a shower, complained about the cold water and was surprised by a sympa-thetic response from a neighbor in his own shower on the other side of the wall. Such enforced togetherness was great fun for a child who had spent so much time with imaginary playmates, and the children in MacLachlan's novels are never wanting for close friends and understanding neighbors. When the Pritzkaus moved to their own house, it was in the country not far from the small school MacLachlan attended. Nearby was a small library where she spent a great deal of time (and enjoyed the illusion that the library was her personal possession).

In 1956, MacLachlan graduated from Windham High School in Willimantic, Connecticut, and went on to the University of Connecticut, where she majored in English education. In the mid-dle of her college years, however, she temporarily dropped out of school, moved to New York City, and took a job as a service repre-sentative for Prentice Hall Publishers in Englewood Cliffs, New Jersey. At the time she had no thought of becoming a writer, and she would later look back on this early dabbling in the publishing world as pure coincidence. In fact, her job at Prentice Hall had lit-tle to do with writing, although it gave her the opportunity to observe the publishing world firsthand. She was, as she puts it, "biding my time," and the years in New York brought her a new sense of purpose so that she returned to the University of Con-necticut with a more mature perspective and serious determina-tion. She remains a strong believer in the value of real-world expe-rience for college students, and her children all opted to delay their college educations in order to work, travel, and generally sort out their lives before pursuing a degree. Even though she was an English major, MacLachlan did virtually no college writing aside from classroom assignments. As always, though, she read extensively. Her career as a writer was not a deliberate forward movement but a series of loosely connected experiences that would move her in fits and starts toward a goal of which she had but a vague notion.

She received her baccalaureate from the University of Connecticut in 1962 and was married on April 14 of the same year to Robert MacLachlan, a clinical psychologist. Immediately upon her graduation, she took a job as a junior high school English teacher in Manchester, Connecticut. She taught for one year, but it was not a particularly happy experience. She was beset by the normal frustrations that face a first-year teacher: the least-desirable classes, the least-motivated students, and too many of both. Her husband then got a job in a clinic in Bridgeport, Connecticut, and they moved there. His income was adequate to support them without her working, so MacLachlan gave up her teaching career and devoted her time to raising a family. They had three children: two sons, John (born in 1964) and Jamie (born in 1967); and a daughter, Emily (born in 1970). MacLachlan was a full-time mother, just as her own mother had been.

She was only eight when she made her solemn vow *not* to become a writer. Whether due to this vow or simply the natural interruptions of life as a mother and wife, she was fairly successful at *not* writing for many years. But during the early years of her marriage, in the midst of carpooling, music lessons, and PTA meetings, she found herself observing people and events and taking copious notes, filling numerous notebooks over time. As a young mother she served for many years on the board of a local organization in Northampton, Massachusetts, called the Children's Aid Family Services Agency, which was dedicated to helping children and families in trouble. Unlike many boards, this one was actively involved in the day-to-day business of the agency. During her tenure, MacLachlan learned much about the plight of families in trouble, about foster homes, and about the abandonment of children. She wrote a series of newspaper articles on foster mothers as part of her contribution to the agency, and these experiences eventually led to *Mama One, Mama Two*, as well as to the many references to abandoned children (or children fearing abandonment) throughout her novels. This is just one example of how her life experiences have informed her writing. She has remarked in retrospect that during these years as a homemaker and mother, she was preparing to be a writer but did not know it. These were incubation years for MacLachlan: Her keen perceptions of her children and their friends would eventually be resurrected in the rich variety of characters that would people her books.

It was not until her youngest, Emily, entered kindergarten that MacLachlan began writing in earnest. She wrote in the mornings after her husband and children were off to work and school. This gave her the luxury of working without interruptions—although, interestingly, it was not necessarily silence and solitude that she craved. She confesses that she still writes with the television on, providing her with white noise to keep her from being distracted—so accustomed had she become to the constant noise of family about the house. She finds she cannot work to music, perhaps because for MacLachlan, music is not background noise but an experience to be absorbed and enjoyed.

Also, when her children were finally all in school, MacLachlan enrolled in an extension course on writing for children that was taught by Jane Yolen, who would be her first important source of encouragement and a good friend as well. It was Yolen who sent a version of one of MacLachlan's picture-book stories to Craig Virden, an agent who in turn sent it to Charlotte Zolotow. Zolotow, immediately taken by the extraordinary imagery and poetic language, bought the book that was to become *Through Grandpa's Eyes*. By a curious fluke, within virtually the same month, Pantheon bought *The Sick Day*, a manuscript that MacLachlan had been circulating herself without the aid of an agent. And so quite suddenly, in a matter of a few short weeks, the writing career that had been incubating for so many years was well under way.

MacLachlan seems never to have thought of writing anything but books for children. Her deep interest in childhood and her obvious joy in her own children and in motherhood pointed her in the direction of writing for children. Among the first stories she wrote were animal stories. She began with talking-animal stories because she found it less intimidating to put words in the mouths of animals than in the mouths of humans. Fortunately, she overcame this fear, largely as a result of the encouragement of Yolen, who helped her to see that her true subject matter surrounded her every day in the form of her own family and acquaintances, and their experiences. *The Sick Day* grew directly out of one of these experiences. MacLachlan admits to freely using the people she knows, and has known, as sources. Her children, her husband, her parents, her friends—all turn up eventually in one or more of her books. In that respect, Patricia MacLachlan is a more personal writer than most, a more biographical writer. But her own depth and breadth of vision give her work a universality and a richness that belie the apparently limited scope of her subjects and themes. MacLachlan once noted, "For now, as in the past, I can only write about the questions and issues that confront me, that trouble me—the ones that whisper in my ear or . . . threaten me. It is my way, whether by fact or by fiction, of naming my own shadows."[5]

Charlotte Zolotow early on recognized that the picture-book format was too limiting for MacLachlan. She had too much to say to be confined by the 32-page picture book. MacLachlan soon began writing longer works, beginning with the very successful *Arthur, for the Very First Time* in 1980. This, her first novel, was an ALA Notable Book and won the Golden Kite Award for Fiction, the first of many book awards that would be showered on MacLachlan. She dabbled briefly in fantasy (*Moon, Stars, Frogs and Friends* and *Tomorrow's Wizard*—the first a picture book, the second a collection of loosely connected short stories), but her chief interests and strengths were in realistic fiction. Throughout the 1980s she devoted herself to fiction for children in the middle years (from about fourth to sixth grades) and gained celebrity status with *Sarah, Plain and Tall,* which won the Newbery Medal for 1986. *Sarah, Plain and Tall* went on to even greater fame as a Hallmark Hall of Fame television production starring Glenn Close. At the invitation of Close, who had done a reading of the book for Caedmon, MacLachlan wrote the screenplay, adapting the story to a more inclusive audience of both adults and children.

The success of *Sarah* prompted a sequel, *Skylark,* which appeared first as a television film and then ultimately in book format. Her screenplay writing career has continued to flourish. She has since written screenplays for television productions of *Journey* (a novel originally published in 1991), again for the Hallmark series, and for *Baby* (originally published in 1993), for Turner Network Television. She finds writing screenplays exciting—"You never know how they are going to turn out [on the screen]."[6] Her books lend themselves to screen adaptations, for they have a cinematic quality in their series of interconnected incidents. She does find it difficult at times to rewrite the same story from a different point of view, for it requires summoning up once more the inspirational impulse that created the original story. In *Skylark* she was required to take an original screenplay for adults and transform it into a book for children, which meant eliminating material, a process MacLachlan seems not to have found so creatively rewarding and which she claims she does not wish to repeat.

In the mid-1980s, after more than a 20-year absence, she returned to the classroom as an adjunct professor at Smith College, where she taught children's literature. And, of course, as a popular writer she has also been in much demand as a guest of elementary schools—a task she seems to relish and learn from. Eventually, the demands of her writing career made the college teaching impossible and she resigned.

MacLachlan does find writing particularly demanding. For her, composition is largely an internal process: She may mull over a story in her head for a very long time before anything gets written. She is, in fact, known to dislike the actual process of committing words to paper and puts it off as much as possible. Perhaps because of her ambivalent feelings about writing and the highs and lows it brings her, MacLachlan has often written about writers. In her very first book, *The Sick Day*, the househusband-father is a writer. Additionally, Arthur, Cassie Binegar and her friend Jason, Anna Witting, and Minna Pratt's mother are all writers or aspiring writers. A recurring theme in MacLachlan's work is that writers must take pains to avoid becoming introverted, passive observers. The writer, a deeply sensitive individual, must be actively engaged in life and living. MacLachlan's own life reflects her conviction that active engagement in life and human relationships is an essential element in the writer's experience—that the most important things that happen in a writer's life do not happen at the typewriter. Her writing is effective and moving because she has a passionate involvement in what she writes, and her conviction that life is to be lived and not merely observed is a theme of nearly every book.

But by the same token, MacLachlan works long and hard at her craft. She is not a prolific writer and her works are all generally short; she has, in fact, a fondness for the short story, but she has not pursued the form seriously because it lacks a viable market in children's literature. It is quite possible that the brevity of her works (as well as the relatively small number of works) results from her somewhat erratic writing habits. However, we should also note that the episodic construction of her books is perfectly suited to her philosophical view that lives are lived in brief scenes loosely connected by thematic threads (which we are usually unaware of at the time). Her literary structure is meant, therefore, to mirror life as she sees it and should be seen as a deliberate artifice, not a limitation. She labors over every word, and her editors describe her as a perfectionist who submits a manuscript only in a polished format. Most of her editors will acknowledge that with her material, there is very little editing to be done, a tribute to her own consummate artistry. She has, indeed, been fortunate in having editors who have understood her and who have exercised patience with her habit of working in "peaks and valleys," as she describes it. Her editors have chosen not to interfere with her process or to insist on deadlines, for in the words of one editor, "No matter how long it takes, it's always been worth it in the end."[7]

In many respects, it is easy to see Patricia MacLachlan as having had a charmed life. Raised by educated and devoted parents, encouraged in her pursuit of knowledge, wed to a caring and understanding husband, and blessed with lively and engaging children, she was free to pursue her writing almost as a pleasant pastime. And the natural eloquence of her books beguiles us into supposing that their writing was effortless. This is, of course, not the case. There is an ancient Latin proverb that says *Ars est celare artem*, "Art lies in concealing art." The great work of art appears as natural as the flower in spring, and is, perhaps, hardly less miraculous. MacLachlan's gift of language and her passion for people have been happily combined to create books that are both remarkably honed and keenly insightful. When we reflect on MacLachlan's life and work, the words of Eudora Welty are once again called to mind: "As you have seen, I am a writer who came of a sheltered life. A sheltered life can be a daring life as well. For all serious daring starts from within."[8] Some writers look around them and write what they see; others look inward and write what they feel. Patricia MacLachian began her career as the former and has metamorphosed into the latter, and it is a transformation that has left the world of children's literature immeasurably richer.

Chapter Two

The Picture Books and Short-Story Collections

All the places to love are here.

—All the Places to Love

Patricia MacLachlan began her career as a writer of picture books and short stories for the very young. She quickly turned to writing short novels for readers in the middle and upper elementary grades. Only after a decade of writing these novels would she return to writing picture books once again. In the following pages, we will examine her development in the arena of picture books and short stories, keeping in mind that between the first picture book, *The Sick Day*, and the last, *What You Know First*, some 16 years and eight novels intervene.

Most of her picture books dispense with plot lines altogether and consist instead of a series of interrelated images evoking the narrator's or the protagonist's response to the world. Her early picture books are, as might be expected, experimental, and each is quite different from the other in structure, narrative point of view, and theme. Her later picture books are all of a kind, historical in their setting, heavily reliant on description of nature, and romantic, even nostalgic, in tone. It is as if she found her voice and settled on her purpose in these later books. They are self-assured, deeper, more thoughtful works. She turns entirely to the first-person narrator in these books, which gives them an intensely personal aura. They are all based to a significant degree on MacLachlan's own childhood experiences. Her language becomes increasingly poetic as she sharpens her focus on images and as her ear—always good—captures a still more graceful lyricism.

Tomorrow's Wizard and *Seven Kisses in a Row* are identified as short-story collections, although they possess a distinct unity in characters, theme, and even chronology that tempts us to see them as novellas. Unlike the novels, these books are intended for readers in the primary grades, and the individual chapters are far more self-contained. MacLachlan has not produced anything similar since; they appear to be anomalies among her published works. Nevertheless, they clearly show her penchant for the episodic style, her emphasis on character development, and her wry humor.

Picture Books

The Sick Day

After attempting animal stories and receiving publishers' rejections for over a year, MacLachlan wrote *The Sick Day* (1979), a realistic story based on a factual account of her husband and daughter. It was accepted by Pantheon within the same month that *Through Grandpa's Eyes* (1980) was accepted by Charlotte Zolotow at Harper. *The Sick Day* was illustrated by the famed illustrator, William Pene du Bois, himself a Newbery Medalist for his fantasy *Twenty-One Balloons*. It was a considerable coup for MacLachlan to have landed not only a respected publisher but also a widely known illustrator for her first venture into children's books. Despite the very personal background of the story, MacLachlan points out that the du Bois illustrations of the father and daughter in no way resemble anyone in her family. It is a book in small format, which is especially suited to MacLachlan's delicate touch, and the motifs and themes in the story are those that continue to dominate MacLachlan's writing.

The story is about a little girl named Emily (for MacLachlan's own daughter) who has fallen ill and places an endless string of demands on her father, a writer, who must care for her while Mother is away at work. The book opens with a now clichéd complaint from Emily: "I have a stomach ache in my head." (Almost the exact epithet was recently used in a popular family motion picture.) Emily says she also has a "headache in my throat" and that her "toe hurts where I stubbed it last year." From her very first published work, MacLachlan reveals her interest in language

and its nuances. The humor in *The Sick Day* often rises from
Emily's creative use of language. Emily describes a hurt on her
toe: "It hurts on and off. The ons are long." When her stomach
feels queasy, she announces, "I think I have to swallow up." And
Father also engages in the wordplay in this exchange:

> "I'm hungry," whined Emily. . . .
> "What do you feel like?" asked Father.
> "A cucumber sandwich with mayonnaise."
> "That's funny," said Father. "You don't look like a cucumber
> sandwich with mayonnaise."

Of course, it is not the humor that is remarkable about these
passages but the tender father-daughter relationship MacLachlan portrays. The next day, the story concludes, Father falls ill,
and now Mother must remain home from work to care for him.
MacLachlan is not ready to wholly dismantle traditional roles—
nor will she ever be, for family life in its myriad forms is crucial
to society as she views it. Certainly, *The Sick Day* seems today
very much in the mainstream, but in 1979, children's books,
always much more conservative and restrained than their adult
counterparts, adhered quite closely to traditional role models.
Mothers stayed home to keep the house and take care of sick
children; mothers were most often seen interacting with their
daughters; and fathers, when they were not working, tended to
their sons. So in choosing to portray a father who remains at
home (he is a writer) and a mother who goes off to work,
MacLachlan is deliberately challenging customary gender roles.
Throughout her writing, MacLachlan stubbornly refuses to con-
form to traditional social expectations; her books are filled with
women who abhor housekeeping, men who are overtly sensitive,
and brothers and sisters who actually demonstrate their love for
each other.

Along with a sensitive portrayal of human relationships, we can
always count on a celebration of art in some manifestation or
another in every MacLachlan book. In *The Sick Day*, we see art
introduced in the form of literature, drawing, and music (there is

no television operating in this home). Father writes, plays the recorder (music is present in virtually everything MacLachlan writes), and draws pictures; Emily makes up both poems and songs, reads voraciously, and draws pictures. Emily's poem about the three comical ponytails her father puts in her hair readily conveys her joy:

> I look like a fountain,
> And I look like me.
> I look beautiful
> In my ponytails three.

Later, Emily asks her father to paint her a picture of a monster "to scare the bug away." He complies with a drawing of a "rose-colored monster with wide teeth and a daisy in his hand." The picture makes Emily smile. And when Father is sick, Emily entertains him by drawing pictures. One of the boons of music as an art form is that its creation and enjoyment can be a communal experience. So while father plays a tune on the recorder, Emily makes up a song to go with it. MacLachlan, who seldom writes down to her audience, even manages to work in the name of Bach. Classical music is a passion of MacLachlan's, and references to music and musicians are fairly common throughout her work. Music serves as a perfect image for MacLachlan's conviction that art is a source of both pleasure and self-expression. In *The Sick Day* we see art being used both to pass the time pleasurably and to communicate emotions in ways for which words alone might be inadequate (Emily's poetry, for example, serves these dual purposes of pleasure and sharing feelings).

The Sick Day has proved a durable book, and the publishers have plans to reissue it with new illustrations. Because the du Bois illustrations were sold after his death, it was impossible to reuse them. Instead, the publishers decided to recast the pictures with a multicultural emphasis. That this could be imagined without distorting the story suggests the universality of the work—and this too is characteristic of much of MacLachlan's writing.

Through Grandpa's Eyes

Through Grandpa's Eyes, published in the same year, focuses specifically on the theme of understanding others. This was MacLachlan's first book with Harper, and she was fortunate enough to have Charlotte Zolotow as her first editor there. On seeing the manuscript of *Through Grandpa's Eyes*, Zolotow noted that it contained beautiful observations, striking imagery, and a passionate zeal for living. What it lacked, however, was structure, which Zolotow helped MacLachlan supply by imposing a chronological sequencing on the events (MacLachlan's early works, including the two collections of short vignettes, *Tomorrow's Wizard* and *Seven Kisses in a Row*, tend to lack tightly knit structural patterns). *Through Grandpa's Eyes* is the first-person narrative of John, a little boy who acts as eyes for his blind grandfather. On the very first page, the concept of seeing things as others see them is introduced: "[Grandpa] doesn't see the house the way I do. He has his own way of seeing." Then we are told how the sun rouses John with its light but awakens Grandpa with its warmth. MacLachlan seems deliberately to be tearing away at stereotypes of the handicapped, for Grandpa is, aside from his sightlessness, a fine physical specimen, engaging in the early morning in strenuous exercise that far exceeds John's capabilities.

Grandpa's compensating sense of smell is demonstrated; not only can he forecast what is cooking for breakfast but he can also identify flowers by their smell. His skill amazes John: "How can Grandpa tell? All the smells mix together in the air." With equal amazement, John observes Grandpa handily moving through the house along his "smooth path." After breakfast, Grandpa and John go to the living room to play their cellos—always the music. Here MacLachlan manages to work in a brief string lesson: "My fingering hand slides up and down the cello neck—toward the pegs for flats, toward the bridge for sharps."

Other art forms appear in the narrative, as well. Nana is sculpting a bust of Grandpa, and Grandpa shows John how to "see" the sculptured head with his hands. In language perhaps a bit too poetic for such a youthful narrator, John describes the experience: "My waterfall fingers flow down his clay head, filling in the spaces beneath the eyes like little pools before they flow down over the cheeks." And John agrees that "It does feel like Grandpa." This is a preview of the lyricism that has come to characterize much of MacLachlan's writing.

Then John and his grandfather go for a walk to the river, where Grandpa recognizes the birds by their calls, blackbirds along the riverbank and geese in the sky above. Together John and Grandpa smell the breezes and feel the wet earth beneath their feet. After they wash and dry the lunch dishes, Grandpa, Nana, and John all take their books outside to read, Grandpa reading Braille. When he laughs out loud at an amusing passage that Nana begs him to share, we come to understand reading Braille as a very normal activity. The day concludes quietly, as it began, with some television (Grandpa listens, of course), and Grandpa takes John up to bed to tuck him in. John and Grandpa exchange comments from their bedrooms, and it is Nana who instructs John to go to sleep. And although her voice sounds stern, John knows that it is smiling at him: "I know. Because I'm looking through Grandpa's eyes."

In its uneventfulness, the book is full of subtle messages aimed at showing us not only how the blind function in everyday life but also how the blind share the same joys and wonders as the sighted. Once again MacLachlan is ahead of her time in writing a sensitive story of an individual with a disability—and showing us that it is, in fact, no disability. There is no pity and Grandpa shows no regret. His attitude is one of positive acceptance. The book proclaims a joyful and serene affirmation of life. By using a grandfather and grandson, MacLachlan is able to present one of her favorite themes, the rich intergenerational relationships that can develop between the very young and the very old. Similar relationships are found throughout her later books. *Through Grandpa's Eyes* is a story of love and of the enjoyment of life, which transcends age and physical limitations. The illustrations by Deborah Ray use a naïve style that is suited to the point of view of the child narrator and quite beautifully complement the story. It is a book filled with many and varied forms of beauty, the beauty made of human efforts—music, sculpturing, and literature—and the beauty inherent in nature—the flora, the fauna, and the landscape. MacLachlan imbues the story with a gentle humor and a passion for the simple things in life, qualities that appear in all her finest works.

Moon, Stars, Frogs, and Friends

Published in the same year as *Arthur, for the Very First Time,* her first book for older readers, *Moon, Stars, Frogs, and Friends* (1980) represents MacLachlan's first experiment with fantasy. It is also a more broadly comical book than she is accustomed to writing, her humor typically being gentler and subtler. The whimsical text is happily matched by Tomie de Paola's lighthearted cartoon illustrations. It is the story of a lonely frog, Randall, who is unsuccessful in making friends. His hopes are raised when he meets Rupert, a pale green frog, who is actually a prince turned into a frog by the "foxy-looking witch" Esme. The spell was the result of Esme's poor reading skills, for she had wished to turn Rupert into a fine musician instead (Rupert is a cellist with "no sharps and flats"). Randall tries to make the most of the new friendship, teaching Rupert to enjoy "the moon, stars, and being friends," but Rupert begins to miss Esme. Finally, to satisfy his friend, Randall goes out in search of Esme. When he finds her, he explains Rupert's predicament (she was unaware of the unfortunate spell she cast). Esme discovers that it takes the kiss of a princess to undo the spell. Fortunately, just at that moment, a plump princess with a wide, smiling mouth, comes along, and Esme persuades her to kiss Rupert. The magic works and Rupert is returned to his former state, but the wide-mouthed princess is now a frog, and she has eyes for Randall. Rupert and Esme are married and have 14 daughters, and Randall and the princess are married and have 444 little frogs, the youngest of whom is adept at singing French rounds. A grateful Rupert comes daily to the pond to play his cello for Randall.

At times within the book, MacLachlan moves into a parody of the folktale form, but she retains too much of the spirit of the traditional folktale form to successfully accomplish this purpose. Nor does it seem likely that parody was her motive. The result is a somewhat awkward updating of the magical transformation story, with a rather heavy-handed message about the value of friendship and the importance of the simple things in life. But other messages within the book are not so clear. Esme's character is elusive—she is "foxy-looking" but apparently incompetent as a witch. The fact that her incompetence derives from her poor reading skills seems to be another heavy-handed message about the importance of learning. Readers are apt to be puzzled over this amalgam of the beautiful princess and the bungling, illiterate sorceress. Perhaps MacLachlan has created a more complex character than the brief folktale can contain, and the result is more perplexing than satisfying—we simply do not understand Esme or her purpose. And the reason for Randall's failure to make friends is quite inexplicable, for he is portrayed as utterly charming. It is even more disturbing to think that possibly it is Randall's intellectual bent that has prevented him from having close friends—is he another version of the "geek" or "nerd," to use the lingo of today's youth?

The principal flaw is that MacLachlan builds the plot around the message rather than allowing the message to arise from the story. A similar flaw is found in her fantasy for older readers, *Tomorrow's Wizard,* which was her last attempt at fantasy before she settled happily into the arena of realistic fiction, a move that proved both wise and fruitful. We should not overlook the fact that, although *Moon, Stars, Frogs, and Friends* may not entirely succeed as sound fantasy, it is imbued with the same warmth and human compassion that we come to expect from MacLachlan's work. Nor should we overlook the wisdom—the primacy of loving relationships, the joy of family life, and the importance of music in life as a means of communicating human emotion. If some of its messages are mixed, the overall effect, enhanced by the colorful cartoons of Tomie de Paola, is a curious combination of nonsense and serene reflection—just as the title suggests. We often get much less from picture books.

Mama One, Mama Two

Mama One, Mama Two (1982) was MacLachlan's last picture book for nearly a decade. This is the story of a little girl, Maudie, who is living with a foster mother, Katherine—"Mama Two"—while her own mother, "Mama One," recuperates in an institution, presumably from a mental breakdown. Inspired by MacLachlan's work on the board of the Children's Aid Family Services Agency, where she developed an interest in foster families, the subject is a bold one for any child's book but almost astonishing for a picture book. The narrative is tenderly presented as a story within a story. Maudie, unable to sleep, looks in on Katherine's baby, who has begun to cry. When Katherine comes into the room, Maudie says, "Tell me the story again. . . . The story about Mama One, Mama Two." Katherine suggests that they tell the story together, and Maudie begins, "Once upon a time . . ." We learn that Maudie's mother was an artist, and in the beginning, she and Maudie (who refers to herself in the third person in the embedded narrative) shared a very happy relationship. Maudie particularly remembers their curling up "like spoons" beneath a quilt and enjoying the bright pictures her mother used to paint of trees with yellow birds and sunsets.

But then her mother sank into a depression (or "became unhappy," as the text puts it). She withdrew into her room and was unable to cook, clean, or even care for Maudie, who had only crackers to eat for breakfast and spent her days in loneliness. Finally, Mama One sought help from a social worker who recommended that she be institutionalized and Maudie placed temporarily in a foster home. This potentially devastating experience is couched in delicate terms. The social worker tells Maudie that her mother's absence is like that of the bluebird's when it flies away for the winter: "But the bird will come back in the spring. And maybe your Mama will, too." Maudie's home with Katherine has brought new joys: She cares for the baby, learns to make pancakes, and makes new friends, and one friend even says she is lucky because she has two mamas. The story within the story ends, and the baby has finally fallen asleep. Katherine crawls into bed next to Maudie, and they curl up "like spoons" under the quilt, just as Maudie and her own mother used to do.

The embedded narrative is a technique that MacLachlan uses again, most effectively in *Unclaimed Treasures*. It works especially well in *Mama One, Mama Two* because we are assured from the very beginning that Maudie is all right; our anxiety over her well-being is relieved. But MacLachlan may have had another motive in using this narrative style, for as Maudie tells her part of the story, she adds details she has never included before. Katherine remarks, "I never heard the crackers part of the story." Later on, Maudie chides Katherine for not letting her tell her part of the story: "Let me tell it. . . . That's the girl's story." The narrative process is part of the therapeutic process. In telling the story, Maudie is able to come to terms with it rather than suppress it, which might be a normal reaction. Recalling details she had not included before is therefore a sign of her acceptance of her circumstances, perhaps even a limited understanding.

Many writers might have succumbed to the temptation to close the book with Mama One's homecoming. MacLachlan prefers to close it with reasonable hope but with no promises and no miracles. The story is told with great sensitivity and is filled with the crisp and simple images that MacLachlan continues to use so effectively—the paintings of trees filled with yellow birds and of sunsets; the bluebirds perched on telephone wires just before they begin their flight south; mother and daughter curled beneath a warm quilt. The imagery is gentle and warm, and it establishes the tone for the story, removing fear and anxiety. We are nevertheless quite aware of the mature nature of the subject. It is easy to understand Charlotte Zolotow's sentiment when she evaluated MacLachlan's early work: "She had so much to say; it would be easier to expand than contract, as you must in a picture book. I thought something longer would give her more freedom. Her unusual but complex thoughts needed room to unfold. . . ."[1] With *Mama One, Mama Two,* it was becoming clear that MacLachlan was ready to move into a longer format and to write for an older audience in order to explore the complex ideas that so compelled her.

Three Names

After a hiatus of nine years, MacLachlan returned to the picture book format with the lovely *Three Names* (1991). Perhaps encouraged by her success with historical fiction in *Sarah, Plain and Tall*, MacLachlan set this story on the prairie sometime near the turn of the century. It is about a stray dog who comes to the farm of the narrator's great-grandfather. The dog is called Three Names because Papa called him Pal, Mama called him Boots, and sister Lily called him Ted. Great-grandfather called him Three Names—"That's four names," the young narrator points out, "but he already knew that" (8). Three Names becomes part of the family and particularly enjoys accompanying the children to their one-room school.

The story is very simple and virtually plotless, chronicling a single year in the childhood of the narrator's great-grandfather, and the chronological arrangement, as one reviewer has pointed out, "lends symmetry as it underscores the relationship between the cycle of the school year and the cycle of the seasons."[2] Three Names is given a lively personality—he likes all the children at school except for sly William at whom he "always frowned"; he barks at the wildlife he sees and even "at a cloud that covered the sun" (15). And at the winter holidays party, when Martha played her fiddle, "Three Names lifted his head to howl at the rafters" (24). The gentle humor seems especially appropriate to the character of the youthful narrator; the humor is found in the very kinds of things that are genuinely funny to children. Not all writers of books for young children are adept at this; MacLachlan has been a careful and sensitive observer.

MacLachlan provides a finely detailed portrait of late-nineteenth-century schooling, including the types of lessons, the parties, and the physical surroundings (for instance, in good weather, the children ate lunch outside and played marbles; in the winter, the teacher arrived at school early to build the fire, and no one stayed in the outhouse long; and in the spring, occasional tornadoes forced the children into the safety of the cellar). As we might expect, MacLachlan's depiction of life on the prairie is full of charm. In one of the few books describing school (as has been previously mentioned, she seems much to prefer writing about the activities of summer), she portrays an almost idyllic educational setting. Her narrator tells us in simple but lyrical prose that "A hundred years ago when Great-grandfather was young, summer was fine, full of long, warm days, and nights when the moon rose yellow. But he missed school" (31). And so, we are assured, did Three Names.

This is the first of three picture books to date that consist of MacLachlan's lyrical celebrations of life on the western prairie. In *Three Names*, as in the two picture books that followed, MacLachlan's text is much more assured, her style more mature, and her touch more delicate than we find in the earlier picture books. The poetic quality dominates and is suited perfectly to a series of vignettes she deftly portrays throughout the book. Her description of the barn illustrates her use of images to establish atmosphere as well as the rhythm of her prose: " 'There was a barn, too, for horses, cool and dark, that smelled of hay and harness leather and old wood. It smelled of Jed, Jenny's pinto, gray-dappled Maude, and Sophie with the white blaze face. Mostly,' said Great-grandfather, 'it smelled the old sweet smell of all the years of horses that had ever slept there' " (17). We hear the unmistakable echo of E. B. White in this passage. Compare his description of the barn in *Charlotte's Web*:

> The Barn was very large. It was very cold. It smelled of hay and it smelled of manure. It smelled of the perspiration of tired horses and the wonderful sweet breath of patient cows. It often had a sort of peaceful smell—as though nothing bad could happen ever again in the world. It smelled of grain and of harness dressing and of axle grease and of rubber boots and of new rope. . . . But mostly it smelled of hay, for there was always hay in the great loft up overhead. And there was always hay being pitched down to the cows and the horses and the sheep.[3]

E. B. White is one of the great influences on MacLachlan's writing, most particularly in the matter of style. They share a light touch and a passion for lean, direct sentences. Both have a talent for combining simple wisdom with grace.

Three Names is unabashedly romantic, depicting an earlier, simpler, carefree time when families worked together on the farm and communities were united and strong. Each page evokes beauty and simplicity and security. The watercolor illustrations by the late Alexander Pertzoff are appropriately romantic with luminous colors and a marked impressionistic style. Pertzoff, in preparing the illustrations, worked from photographs he had taken, including some of MacLachlan's grandparents' old farm in North Dakota. And for one illustration depicting a party scene, Pertzoff worked from a photograph he had taken of MacLachlan herself, her husband, her father, and several of her friends, who all dressed in period costumes for the occasion.

All the Places to Love

In the same vein as *Three Names*, *All the Places to Love* (1994) combines MacLachlan's love of family with love of place. It is a first-person narrative of a little boy named Eli who, on the day his sister Sylvie is born, reminisces about his early memories on the farm. The book is a celebration of place, and Eli begins by telling about his birth in the farmhouse, when his grandmother wrapped him in a blanket "made from the wool of her sheep." The setting is a large farm sometime earlier in the century. The time period is vague, although the illustrations depict an idyllic rural setting with a horse-drawn plow, and the clothing seems to date from the 1930s. The illustrations are realistic paintings by Mike Wimmer that have a distinctly Norman Rockwell–like flavor, but without Rockwell's gentle humor.

As with *Three Names*, there is no plot, but rather a series of images recollected by the narrator. The images introduce the various members of Eli's family, and each is associated with that part of the farm he or she loves best. Grandmother loves the river; Papa loves the open fields; Mama loves the hills where she picks blueberries; and Grandfather, who is widely traveled, loves his barn, "where the soft sound of cows chewing [can] make all the difference in the world." The world depicted is one full of life. Cows, sheep, and dogs roam the land; grackles, redwings, and crows fill the skies; and in the river, "trout flashed like jewels in the sunlight." There are also deer and ducks and killdeers and turtles and wild turkeys. The soil is sweet. Eli and his father both put a handful of dirt in their pockets. (MacLachlan, when she visits schoolrooms, carries along her bag of prairie dirt.)

The book is an exquisite collection of carefully drawn images conveyed in soothing lyrical passages. The prose is arranged like poetry on the page, and the following passage describing Grandfather's barn indicates the essentially poetic quality of the language:

> Leather harnesses hang like paintings against old wood;
> And hay dust floats like gold in the air.

MacLachlan delights in the creation of sensitive male figures, and Grandfather and Papa are both depicted in tender moments. The narrative opens with Eli describing the day he was born in the farmhouse, when his grandmother held him up to the window so that he would first see "all the places to love," and his grandfather, on seeing him, cried tears of joy. Eli recalls the joy of being with his Papa and his Papa's sensitivity in this colorful passage:

> Once Papa and I lay down in the field, holding hands,
> And the birds surrounded us:
> Raucous black grackles, redwings,
> Crows in the dirt that swaggered like pirates.

And at the close of the book, when we discover that this is the day that Eli's sister is born, Grandfather once again weeps at the birth of a grandchild.

With each birth, Grandfather carves the name of the new baby on a rafter in the barn alongside the names of the parents and grandparents. This act serves to make them a part of the place they live and is akin to Sarah Witting's writing her name in the dirt to proclaim her loyalty to her new home in *Skylark*. The birth also is a sign of the cycle of life, with things beginning anew and Eli recognizing that his responsibility will be to make sure that Sylvie learns about all the places to love. He happily anticipates the time when

I will carry Sylvie on my shoulders through the fields;
I will send her message downriver in small boats;
And I will watch her at the top of the hill,
Trying to touch the sky.
I will show her my favorite place, the marsh,
Where ducklings follow their mother
Like tiny tumbles of leaves.

What You Know First

The title of *What You Know First* (1995) actually came from a remark made by an elementary-school student in a class MacLachlan was visiting, and it focuses on a central idea running through much of her work: the lasting importance of our childhood experiences in building our character and establishing our values. *What You Know First* is narrated by a young girl who is unhappy about her family's decision to move from their prairie farm to a home near the ocean. The story is set sometime earlier in the century—the Depression years, if we judge from Barry Moser's monochromatic engravings accompanying the text—when a family must abandon its farm in search of a better living elsewhere. The narrator's resistance to the move is similar to the attitudes of many protagonists in MacLachlan's longer works who lament the changes in their lives. However, this is a new theme for a MacLachlan picture book.

The narrator describes all the things she will miss about her home—from "the slough where the pipits feed" to the "snow drifting hard against fences" and "the horses breathing puffs like clouds in the air." She vows to live with the new people "if they'll have me" or in the "tall cottonwood that was small when Papa was small" or at "Uncle Bly's house by the river" or with Mr. Boots the blacksmith who lives in the barn. But her mother tells her that her baby brother would miss her if she stayed and that he needs her to tell him about their prairie home, to keep those memories alive, to sing Uncle Bly's songs. Her papa tells her that "What you know first stays with you." And so she leaves the farm with her family and with her memories:

And I'll try hard to remember the songs,
And the sound of the rooster at dawn,
And how soft the cows' ears are
When you touch them,
So the baby will know
What he knew first.
And so I can remember, too.

It is a sparse book with much of the flavor of her novels. It is the story of our longing for stability and continuity in a world that will not stand still. It is the story of our need for roots, for a past to which we can lay claim. And it is the story of our need to tell our own stories, to keep the past alive, to remind us of who we are, where we came from, and what is truly elemental in life.

It is a nostalgic tale illustrated with rather somber engravings that are heavy in shadows. Like so many of MacLachlan's books, it includes eccentric characters, such as Uncle Bly, who sings his cowboy songs about buffalo, cattle drives, lightning storms, and love and eats pie for breakfast because he like it, "And no one tells him he can't." And it is a lyrical tale written, like *All the Places to Love*, with attention to the poetic line and rhythm. And it relies on sharp and crystalline imagery—visual (the prairie is an "ocean of grass"), auditory (the rattling of the Cottonwood leaves when it's dry), and tactile (the softness of the cows' ears).

Since Cheyenne is mentioned in the book (one of the few specific place names mentioned in any of MacLachlan's books), we may reasonably assume the farm is located in Wyoming. Wyoming, of course, was MacLachlan's birthplace, and she too left the prairie when she was a girl of four or five, much like the narrator. This is MacLachlan writing about what she knew first, and the book reflects her strong feeling for the land and the importance of the landscape in defining who we are. Even the illustrations emphasize the deeply personal nature of this book, for Moser based his work on old family photographs of MacLachlan's, a fitting tribute to the theme. The narrator will take her memories with her and they will always be a part of her, just as MacLachlan's memories of the Western prairies remained with her and eventually surfaced in some of her most memorable works, including *Sarah, Plain and Tall* and *Skylark*. What further testament do we need to validate her convictions about the landscape?

The later picture books do not explore the social concerns that interested MacLachlan earlier in her career—a child living with a blind grandfather, a father caring for his sick daughter, a child living in a foster home because of her mother's mental illness. Instead, her later picture books focus on the broader, if less topical, themes—the impact of time and change, the importance of the past, the value of human relationships, and the strength of the family. The later picture books also have a timeless quality much like many of her novels, set in an idyllic landscape in the indeterminate past, bathed in nostalgia. Their appeal is a romantic one. The vignettes MacLachlan portrays are decidedly of a bygone era—or more probably of an era that never existed outside the hopeful writer's imagination. But this is not to disparage the loveliness of these works. In writing the novels, MacLachlan discovered her voice, which she then employed in her subsequent picture books. *Three Names*, *All the Places to Love*, and *What You Know First* all give us a vision of childhood as we might wish it to be. And they are lifted from the purely sentimental through the beauty of their language and the depth of their humanity. We should hope that the sentiments expressed in the books, a belief in the strength of the family and the importance of place as an anchorage in our lives, are not so old-fashioned that they no longer hold meaning for today's children.

Short-Story Collections

Tomorrow's Wizard

MacLachlan's first departure from the picture-book format was *Tomorrow's Wizard*, a series of six vignettes about an irascible wizard called Tomorrow, his buoyant apprentice, Murdoch, and a friendly talking horse. The stories grew out of a conversation MacLachlan had with her own children and may have been unconsciously influenced by Natalie Babbitt's *Devil's Storybook*. MacLachlan acknowledges her debt to Babbitt in her clean, sparse prose style, and *The Devil's Storybook*, also a series of vignettes about an irascible character (the Devil himself), contains a satiric humor similar to that in *Tomorrow's Wizard*. But they are very different stories. MacLachlan's wizard is charged with screening people's wishes (and curses) and answering the important ones. The apprentice Murdoch is attempting to acquire these skills, but not without some difficulty. Murdoch keeps forgetting about wizards, since he spends "so much time among humans listening for important wishes." Tomorrow warns him that "There's only a fine line between wizards and humans. If you are not careful you'll forget about becoming a wizard" (3). Later on, Murdoch laments to the horse that wizards are not born, "They just come about, like the sunset or a snowfall," but Murdoch wishes he could be born. "I think being born must be heavenly" (10). Thus the Pinocchio theme—that is, the desire to become human—is introduced subtly. Tomorrow, piqued by the prattle of Murdoch and the horse, causes an entire week to pass by in an instant (to relieve himself of a hastily uttered vow of silence), only to discover that a week's worth of wishes has accumulated to which he must attend. The remaining short stories are ostensibly the tales of those wishes and their outcomes.

The first important wish comes from the father of Rozelle, who wants a husband for his daughter. Rozelle, however, is the most disagreeable maiden in the land, a girl with a generally ugly disposition who is given to temper tantrums. Tomorrow's efforts to find her a husband are futile, as the crotchety Rozelle finds fault with every suitor sent to her. Finally, Murdoch hits upon the notion of introducing Rozelle to the giant who has been habitually plaguing the neighborhood. They are a perfect match, two lonely people with similar natures who find beauty in each other. Because of her, the giant ceases to harass the villagers, and because of the giant, Rozelle acquires a sweet temper. They live happily ever after.

The second important wish involves a thoroughly disagreeable miller, a scoundrel and a cheat (he is called Three-D, for "Dreadful, Dastardly Demon"), and his wife, the homely and equally nasty Mona. They live together miserably with a wretched cat named Clifford. Murdoch, to do them a good turn, takes their ill-tempered cat in exchange for a sweet child named Primrose. Primrose changes their lives: They acquire social graces and friends, their house becomes immaculate, and their days are well-ordered and civil, but they soon discover they are miserable. They long to be like their former selves. But not even Tomorrow will trade the wretched cat Clifford for the sickeningly sweet Primrose. It is Clifford who is able to change Primrose, however. The cat claws her, drawing blood, and she turns suddenly into a little demon herself, shouting ugly names at the cat and finally flinging him across the cottage. The miller and his wife are thrilled at the new Primrose and they decide "All is well." The four of them "lived happily grousing, growling and grumbling ever after" (40).

The third tale is the story of the beautiful Geneva who wishes that men would love her for herself and not her fair face. Tomorrow creates for her a very large nose in order to make her ugly, and as we might predict, the young men of the village "fled in pairs and threes, east and west." Geneva, in her loneliness, has only the animals for her friends. Then one day, a painter named Eric discovers her feeding sparrows from her hand and, seeing her inner beauty, draws a portrait of her with the birds. He courts her and soon asks for her hand in marriage. She realizes that he has never noticed her huge nose, and it does not even appear in his drawing.

Next is the story of a fiddle maker, Bliss, who longs to make the perfect fiddle. Tomorrow, tired of Bliss's constant complaining, decides to grant the wish, but as with his attempts to find Rozelle a husband, his efforts again fail. At last, Tomorrow turns to Bliss's wife, Maude, and urges her to ask Bliss if he thinks she is the perfect wife. When Maude asks the question Bliss responds promptly, "By heavens, no. What would any man wish with a perfect wife? If you were perfect, all our marriage woes would fall on *my* head" (66). And, at that moment Bliss realizes, too, that "no one . . . would want a perfect fiddle either. For the sour notes would be the fault of the fiddler." After that, Bliss is content.

The book ends with "The Last Important Wish." Tomorrow surveys his work along with the High Wizard, a rather comical figure who leans over a cloud far above and grasps a tin tankard, which he rattles when he wants Tomorrow's attention. The High Wizard points out that one wish remains unfulfilled—the faithful horse, who has been a constant companion and sometime assistant since the beginning of the story, "longs for a kind master and a warm barn" (72). So the horse is sent to Farmer Mirth, who discovers that no one can ride him. Farmer Mirth's wife then wishes for someone to be sent who can ride him. At once a baby appears, smiling and happy, wrapped in soft blankets and lying in a basket. It is, of course, Murdoch, who has finally gotten his own wish, leaving Tomorrow not a little sad.

Tomorrow's Wizard has much in common with MacLachlan's first fantasy, *Moon, Stars, Frogs, and Friends*. Despite their folktale elements—a setting vaguely distant in time and place, an emphasis on action, a sparseness of detail, and an unquestioned acceptance of magic—these stories have decidedly modern twists with their often flippant tone and the satirical jibes that create much of their humor. They also contain a poignancy seldom found in the traditional folktale, particularly in their gentle portrayal of affectionate characters. *Tomorrow's Wizard* was generally praised by reviewers. Jane Yolen called it "highly entertaining . . . A real charmer."[4] Another reviewer showered the book with enthusiasm: "A quietly stunning book . . . A book that should stand permanently on every child's shelf."[5] Not all critics were as generous in their assessments; Jerry Spiegler, reviewing the book in the *School Library Journal*, noted that "the message at the heart of these stories is sometimes handed over a bit too easily."[6]

It is true that MacLachlan's fantasies often include rather overt moralizing, which, coupled with the broader humor she employs, can produce awkward results. For example, in the story of Geneva—which is an inverted Beauty and the Beast tale—the intended message is that beauty is within. However, the ridiculing of large noses may be misinterpreted by young readers. Eric, whose love for Geneva blinds him to her physical appearance, paints her portrait replacing her large nose with one that is much more petite. This might imply to some readers that smaller noses are, in fact, preferable. The message might have been more satisfactory had Eric found a certain noble beauty in Geneva's nose, so that her nose, rather than being an imperfection, would become an asset.

Indeed, a predominant theme in both fantasies, *Moon, Stars, Frogs, and Friends* and *Tomorrow's Wizard*, is that imperfections are an inevitable part of life. MacLachlan's characters live happily ever after not because they are perfect (like Cinderella and Prince Charming) but because they have learned to accept their own flaws. Three-D the miller and his family discover they are much happier being miserable and grousing than being superficially polite. The fiddle maker Bliss actually learns that there is some value to imperfection—it allows us to shift the blame from ourselves. However, astute readers are likely to question these messages and the values they espouse. Is it really all right to be happy being miserable? Do imperfections exist so we can have someone or something to blame when things go wrong? The messages are not typical of MacLachlan; they are both too stinging and too negative. Further, the humor is sometimes strained (is the false nose that Geneva wears truly funny?), and the resolutions come too quickly and with too little motivation.

MacLachlan was still clearly experimenting in this work, and she seems not entirely comfortable with the literary fairy tale as a genre. The fable format she chose for *Tomorrow's Wizard* is much better at conveying ideas than exploring character. But her interests are in people and in relationships rather than in ideas. MacLachlan herself once said, "All my books seem to concern themselves with family, who we are as people."[7] Consequently the literary fairy tale too readily allowed her to fall into didacticism and inhibited her drawing of genuine characters. She has written no work of fantasy since *Tomorrow's Wizard*, perhaps because she recognized that, for her, realism would provide a much happier medium.

Despite these weaknesses (and they stand out so sharply only in contrast with the extraordinary works that followed), *Tomorrow's Wizard* does exhibit MacLachlan's deep sense of humanity. In the final story when Tomorrow grants Murdoch his wish to be born a human child, the wizard must stoically bear his loneliness. There is a gentle irony in the wizard who spends his time granting wishes for others being denied what he might wish for himself, the companionship of the protégé whom he has grown to love. It is this feeling of tenderness and poignancy that pervades the work and lingers with us long after the details of the individual stories have faded.

Seven Kisses in a Row

Seven Kisses in a Row (1983) is, like *Tomorrow's Wizard*, a book for early elementary readers consisting of brief stories tied to an over-riding theme. Unlike *Tomorrow's Wizard, Seven Kisses* contains real-istic stories. MacLachlan has said that she loves the short-story format but has been discouraged from pursuing it because, in chil-dren's literature at least, it lacks a viable market. Following *Seven Kisses*, therefore, she resumed writing novels for children in the middle years and picture books. Chronologically, *Seven Kisses* fol-lows her first two novels for middle-aged children, *Arthur, for the Very First Time* and *Cassie Binegar*. By this time, MacLachlan had abandoned fantasy and returned to the realism with which she has always been more comfortable. The protagonist in *Seven Kisses*, an irrepressible girl named Emma, is seven, which is also the approx-imate age of the intended audience. The story of *Seven Kisses* is a slight one: Emma's parents go off to an "eyeball doctors' " con-vention and leave her and her brother Zachary in the care of Aunt Evelyn and Uncle Elliot. The aunt and uncle, who have no chil-dren of their own and apparently have little experience with chil-dren, impose a set of rules on the household, only to discover that rules do not always work when dealing with real people. In short, Emma teaches her aunt and uncle how to be a good aunt and uncle (and good parents, for they are expecting a baby), and Emma herself becomes more adaptable.

The book opens with Emma, an early riser, attempting to wake up her aunt and uncle. When they do not respond (she is not going to get her divided grapefruit with a cherry in the middle or her usual seven kisses in a row from her father), she decides to run away. We soon learn that running away is a harmless routine with Emma. She goes to kindly Mrs. Groundwine's, and her brother

Zachary soon comes to retrieve her. Zachary, who is somewhat older than Emma, proves to be a remarkably sensitive and caring brother (typical of the siblings MacLachlan creates).

Aunt Evelyn and Uncle Elliott attempt to impose many rules on the household, but Emma informs them that she and her brother must follow only three rules: (1) be kind, (2) no kicking or biting, and (3) any rule can be changed. Her aunt and uncle, understanding people, prove to be adaptable. Aunt Evelyn then tells Emma that she is pregnant, and Emma proceeds to offer advice on how to handle babies. Pregnancy plays a key role in many MacLachlan books, and the emphasis is usually on the cycle of life. The precocious Emma sees the new baby as following in her footsteps—in fact, Emma offers an old pair of her baby booties to Aunt Evelyn for her baby.

An entire chapter is devoted to Emma's dawdling over a plate of broccoli. This may be the chapter that one reviewer had in mind when describing the book as too slow paced.[8] Another chapter explores Emma's jealousy over Zachary's girlfriend who comes to visit: "He'll probably show her all his bottle caps! . . . And his dirt collection. I'm the only one who's smelled every jar of his dirt collection" (26). Now it is Aunt Evelyn who gives out the advice, explaining love and marriage to Emma in an attempt to soothe her anxiety over Zachary's girlfriend.

Another episode deals with Emma's refusal to sleep in her room because of the "night rumbles." Aunt Evelyn immediately understands and has her own stories of things that go bump in the night. Emma opts to sleep in a tent in the yard, and before it is all over, the entire family has joined her in the tent. In the penultimate chapter, they clean Emma's terribly cluttered room and learn, in the process, the meaning of "different strokes," the chapter title. It is really a lesson in tolerance, understanding that different people treasure different things and that these differences are perfectly all right.

The final chapter opens with Uncle Elliott waking up Emma and announcing that her divided grapefruit with a cherry and her seven kisses in a row await her. In a reversal of events from the first chapter, Emma calls out, "I'm asleep. . . . Come back later" (49). As it turns out, Emma is faking illness in an attempt to prolong her aunt and uncle's stay. They all have breakfast in bed (which, inexplicably, we discover was never allowed by her otherwise freewheeling parents). Emma gives Uncle Elliott "fathering" lessons using one of her dolls for practice. She teaches him to change diapers and sing lullabies and not to talk baby talk to the baby. Uncle Elliott makes up a lullaby (its music is included at the end of the book); this is the only reference to any art form, unless we count the doggerel recited by Aunt Evelyn that Uncle Elliott wrote for her during their courtship—and it is a stretch to call that verse "art."

Over the course of a few days, Aunt Evelyn and Uncle Elliott have endeared themselves to Emma and Zachary. Everyone has become more tolerant and understanding; however, it appears that Aunt Evelyn and Uncle Elliott have grown the most. We have every confidence by the end of the story that they will be extraordinary parents. This is, indeed, an unusual theme for a book for seven-year-olds.

The book has a decided charm. It has much in common with *The Sick Day,* with its precocious, sometimes wise-cracking little girl and the loving familial relationship portrayed. The humor is similar to that in *The Sick Day* as well, largely derived from the inventive turns of phrase so common to childhood. "We have no lowercase spoons. . . . Only capitals," Emma announces (17). Brother Zach tells Emma she should have eaten her broccoli first "before it got tired out" (19). But it is difficult to sustain a very long book with these sorts of remarks. MacLachlan thus uses the humor of incident—the family members coming one by one to Emma's backyard to keep her company, for example; or Aunt Evelyn knitting a bootie for her baby that ends up fitting Aunt Evelyn.

In many ways, this is a book that may appeal more to an adult than to the intended child audience. The subtle humor and the low-key adventures mingled with some fairly searching conversations are likely to slow the story down for many seven-year-olds. And, as often happens with stories so brief, the moral lessons emerge a bit forcefully. Although in the 1990s she resumed writing picture books, since *Seven Kisses in a Row*, MacLachlan has not written another book for the early elementary reader. The format perhaps proved too confining for her. The picture book, even though it is ostensibly for a younger audience, may have a greater capacity for experimentation on the part of the writer and illustrator than does a chapter book intended for beginning readers. The picture book, with its visual component, has proved quite amenable to MacLachlan's own poetic style, the sparseness of her language being supplemented by the illustrations. MacLachlan's style is also too introspective to provide the kind of action most early elementary children expect from their reading. MacLachlan's picture books, especially her later ones, are the work of a consummate literary artist, and she has been fortunate in finding illustrators who have captured the magic and quiet wonder of her luminous texts.

Chapter Three

The Early Novels: *Arthur, for the Very First Time; Cassie Binegar;* and *Unclaimed Treasures*

It's not easy, this learning how to see the world the way others see it.

—*Cassie Binegar*

Charlotte Zolotow's suggestion that MacLachlan attempt a longer work to allow her "unusual but complex thoughts needed room to unfold" proved to be excellent advice.[1] At this writing she has produced eight novels, all of which are accomplished works of art. Her novels are brief—most are in the neighborhood of 100 to 130 pages—and are directed to an audience of children around the ages of 10 to 12 (*Sarah, Plain and Tall* and its sequel, *Skylark,* are aimed at a slightly younger audience). She drew on the strengths of her best early picture books, *Through Grandpa's Eyes* and *Mama One, Mama Two,* and created in her longer works character studies of individuals facing personal crises typical of preadolescents. Each of the early novels is a third-person narrative written from the point of view of the protagonist. The settings are rural and in the not-too-distant past, and the protagonist is surrounded by a cast of delightfully eccentric characters who help him or her to achieve greater self-awareness, which in turn helps to resolve the crisis. MacLachlan's novels are ostensibly realistic, but it is more accurate to call them romances, for they portray the world as we might wish it to be. It is not a world devoid of sorrow or misfortune, but there is ample love to cushion the blows of fate and sufficient beauty to give us hope for the future. As the following pages will illustrate, her novels, though episodic in structure, are tightly knit through their imagistic patterns, recurring motifs, and interwoven themes, and her bare-bones prose scarcely wastes a syllable.

Arthur, for the Very First Time

Patricia MacLachlan's first novel for older readers, *Arthur, for the Very First Time*, was published in 1980. The book was named an ALA Notable Book and received critical praise for its warm humor, colorful characters, and polished writing style. This is the story of Arthur Rasby, a 10-year-old who is having a problem summer: His parents argue during the day and whisper loudly at night, the house is plagued with plumbing problems that perplex the plumber (who is a woman; MacLachlan was politically correct before it was fashionable), and moles corrupt the Rasby lawn. However, the root of all the problems, so far as Arthur is concerned, is that his mother is going to have a baby, an event that has obviously upset the household and threatens to undermine Arthur's unique position in the family, for he has been an only child. Finally, his parents decide that Arthur should spend his summer with Great-Aunt Elda and Great-Uncle Wrisby, ostensibly so he will not be bored at home, but Arthur cannot shake the feeling that he is not wanted at home. Quietly Arthur goes on this journey of self-discovery.

Almost immediately he is overwhelmed by his aunt and uncle's house and its extraordinary inhabitants. The house itself is alive, mysteriously exciting and inviting; it "reached back over the land like someone stretching, its wings on either side like arms thrown back" (7). Uncle Wrisby is tall and angular, hard of hearing but an expert lip-reader; Aunt Elda is warm and gregarious, "shaped like an uncertain circle, made up of large shifting spaces like an easy-to-color coloring book" (7). These two characters are based loosely on MacLachlan's own parents. Her mother, she recalls, was a plump woman who wore her long hair braided, pinned on top of her head, and set in place with combs. These combs would turn up everywhere, "in the car, beneath the cushions of the couch."[2] MacLachlan's father was a gardener who planted, like Uncle Wrisby, onions and roses. But perhaps more important, MacLachlan credits her father with teaching her how to look at things—or, rather, teaching her that there is more than one way to look at the world, which is exactly what Arthur learns from Uncle Wrisby (with the added insight of Aunt Elda). Not the least extraordinary of the inhabitants is the pet chicken Pauline, who responds only when spoken to in French (as if her responding to human language were itself not extraordinary enough).

Uncle Wrisby and Aunt Elda reveal their peculiar but inviting qualities quite early to Arthur. Uncle Wrisby shows Arthur to his room and shares a pair of binoculars with him, noting that he can look through both ends of the binoculars and see things quite differently. Arthur, a very literal-minded boy, is puzzled by Uncle Wrisby's habit of looking through the big end of the binoculars, the end that makes things appear far away: "Why would anyone want to look through the far away end?" (16). Aunt Elda, on her visit to Arthur's room, introduces him to her pet mockingbird. Arthur watches uneasily as Aunt Elda climbs out of his window and leaves some of her own hair in the tree for the mockingbird to use in its nest. She then reads to him Randall Jarrell's poem, "The Mockingbird," which begins, "Look one way and the sun is going down, / Look the other and the moon is rising" (22). There is always more than one way of looking at things. The binoculars provide us with two visions of the world, as does Jarrell's poem. Arthur's vision of the world is decidedly myopic and inwardly focused. An awareness of new perspectives is precisely what Arthur needs. For example, Uncle Wrisby introduces Arthur to Bernadette, a pregnant pet sow whom Aunt Elda refers to as "his girl friend" (28). Uncle Wrisby sings love ballads to Bernadette, a practice Arthur finds as peculiar as looking through the faraway end of the binoculars. Arthur's journal entries betray his limited imagination and his inability to adopt alternative perspectives: "Uncle Wrisby sang that song about maidens to old fat Bernadette. I don't think Bernadette is any ye fair and tender maiden. And I know my mother wouldn't like me sitting in the mud" (29).

Arthur then meets Moira MacAvin, the granddaughter of the local vet, himself a curious character called Moreover from his habit of speaking in continuous sentences linked with the adverbial conjunction "moreover." Moira and her grandfather both have wild black hair, and they remind Arthur of starlings, "rumpled, unkempt and raucous" (31). Moira is frank, outspoken, and, at times, outrageous—in short, she is exactly the influence Arthur needs to shake him from his complacency and bring him out of his shell. When he befriends a tiny rodent who has made its home in the backseat of Moreover's dilapidated car, Moira nicknames him "Mouse," an epithet clearly intended to reflect Moira's opinion of Arthur's diffidence, his chosen role of passive observer. And Moira perversely insists on calling him Mouse, even though Arthur patiently corrects her by reiterating "Arthur" each time. It is Moira who first questions Arthur about his writing. When Arthur tells her that "I write the things I think about—the things that happen to me," she responds, "Maybe . . . you ought to try making something up for a change. Sometimes it's more interesting." To that, Arthur points out, "But it's not real then." Moira scoffs, "Oh, real . . . What's real?" (39). This, of course, recalls the mockingbird poem for Arthur. Moira continues to be a delightful annoyance for Arthur, forcing him to think about his world in different and sometimes uncomfortable ways. Arthur is impressed, for example, that the MacAvin house is half white, half brown. It has been that way for so long that the MacAvins cannot remember whether Moreover had been painting "a white house brown or a brown house white" (41). This reckless abandon is new to Arthur, whose family assiduously completes every task. The house's interior reflects the same careless, easygoing lifestyle that one would expect from its inhabitants. The striking contrast with Arthur's own life underscores the dichotomy that runs through the book— the binoculars, the mockingbird poem, and the conflict in Arthur's mind between fact and fiction.

When Arthur goes to church with Aunt Elda and Uncle Wrisby, he again sees two perspectives side by side. Aunt Elda is devout, praying to God (whom she refers to as Himself) and carrying on a fierce battle with the devil who is as real to her as her neighbors. Uncle Wrisby sleeps through the sermons and grumbles about having to contribute a whole dollar to the collection. After church, Arthur takes a walk with Moira and observes her pushing her feet into the mud of a pond and sliding her fingers through the plants. "They're the same," Arthur realizes, thinking of Aunt Elda and Moira. "Moira always sits into the earth as if to root there. Aunt Elda becomes part of the bread dough" (48). And it is true that both Moira and Aunt Elda are earth mothers. Their association with the nurturing earth will eventually help Arthur come to terms with his own mother's pregnancy. It is at this time that Moira shares with Arthur the fact that both her parents deserted her, and Arthur responds by saying out loud for the first time in the story, "My mother is going to have a baby" (51). Arthur is disappointed that Moira fails to console him; rather, she responds with characteristic forthrightness and puts the thing into its proper perspective:

> "I don't want to have a baby," said Arthur, suddenly angry.
> "So don't have one"—and she added pointedly, "when you grow up. This one's your parents'." (52)

Moira mercilessly lashes into Arthur: "You spend so much time writing in that journal of yours that you don't really see what's going on around you" (53). Then, she tearfully explains about the frustrating visits she and Moreover receive from the social worker whose job is to determine whether or not Moira should be placed in a foster home. And she confides her doubts about Moreover's love for her, since he has never expressed it openly, and she recalls a time when Moreover told her that it was not good to care for something too deeply, lest it hurt too much when the thing is taken away. Arthur recalls Uncle Wrisby and his wanting to look through the faraway end of the binoculars, for it keeps things at a safe distance. Arthur also recalls his parents' reluctance to tell him outright about the new baby, and he begins to see the danger in just observing. "I'll do something," he tells Moira. "You'll see. I *promise* I'll do something" (55). It is Arthur's first expression of the need to become his own agent—his first step toward self-actualization.

Quite naturally, Bernadette supplies Arthur with his opportunity to prove himself. Arthur begins reading a book that Moira gave him, *When Your Sow Has Babies*. Uncle Wrisby is skeptical, distrustful of books, preferring to rely on nature to see things through. "Don't believe anything written. Only what I see," Uncle Wrisby boasts (14). But Arthur persists and begs to build Bernadette a fenced-off birthing area as the book recommends. Arthur cannot understand Uncle Wrisby's resistance until Aunt Elda points out that "he just doesn't like to know about such things, the bad things that could happen. He figures that if he doesn't know about it, it won't make him worry. Or if he doesn't know about it . . . that maybe it won't happen at all" (59). Arthur at once recognizes that as silly, but he also recognizes the same trait in himself in his refusal to open any of the letters his parents have written him. Not reading their letters prevents the home situation from becoming a reality for Arthur. Finally Uncle Wrisby relents and permits Arthur to build the fenced-in area for Bernadette. When Moreover next visits the farm, he gives his stethoscope to Arthur so he can listen to the babies inside Bernadette's belly. Those "soft and mysterious turnings" have a profoundly moving effect on Arthur, and suddenly he realizes that Bernadette looks different to him now—not so ugly, "almost pleasant" (67). He is able to see Bernadette from a new perspective; he is beginning to acquire a dichotomous vision.

Still one more character is introduced, a huckster named Yoyo Pratt, who comes on Wednesdays with his cart drawn by a contrary donkey he calls Jack the Ass. Yoyo is a bit on the shady side, which apparently justifies Arthur and Uncle Wrisby's attempt to outwit Yoyo. Arthur admires a recorder in its canvas case but finds the $5.00 price tag prohibitive. Arthur instead pays Yoyo $1.00 for the case to store his pencils in, or so he says. Uncle Wrisby then points out to Yoyo that the recorder will likely get damaged without its case, and Arthur offers him $.75 for it. And so Arthur acquires $5.00 worth of merchandise for $1.75. When they later discover that the pet chicken Pauline is missing, that she did not come home with Arthur after he went to show his recorder to Moira, Yoyo's is the first place that Arthur looks. Arthur and Moira find a fowl stewing on the stove. They are sure it is Pauline, that Yoyo has wreaked his revenge for being cheated out of the price of the musical instrument. They steal the pot and its contents and head for Aunt Elda's, where to their amazement, they find Pauline very much alive. Yoyo did not have her after all. The fowl in his pot was a goose, a goose that has now been nosed into the dirt by Bernadette. Arthur and Moira return to Yoyo's home to replace the ruined goose with a chicken that Aunt Elda has been preparing. By a ruse, the substitution is made before the Pratts ever know what happened (at least until supper time). The Yoyo Pratt episode is great fun and is largely a comic diversion before the climax, but it also shows Arthur assuming a more assertive posture.

Following this rollicking episode is a quiet interlude involving Aunt Elda's reminiscence about her Aunt Mag, a story intended to assuage Arthur when, after all his hard work, he discovers that Bernadette appears not to like the pen. Aunt Elda's story is of a mail-order bride, Aunt Mag, who came from the coast of Maine to help care for a widower's children. We learn how she cared for Caleb and loved his children, even when his family scorned her for her peculiar speech and habits. Aunt Elda explains how Aunt Mag took the youngest child into her arms and said, "You won't remember your mother . . . but you will learn that her life touches yours. All of us touch each other. Just like the colors of the prism" (94). This, of course, is the seed of *Sarah, Plain and Tall*. Nested into the narrative of *Arthur,* the story affirms the never-ending link, the interconnectedness of all things, and the mutual dependence we all have on each other. The stepmother's acceptance of her stepchildren helps Arthur to realize his own selfish behavior. Aunt Elda gives Arthur a prism that once belonged to Aunt Mag, which becomes a symbol of the multiple visions, the myriad of perspectives that his summer's experience has furnished him:

> And when Arthur slept that night, his head was filled with many thoughts—of babies, a mockingbird, a nest with long yellow-white hair and short gray hair, a motherless child, a tall woman from Maine and dandelion wine. His thoughts were fused together and criss-crossed, lighting up his dreams.
> Like a prism. (97)

After *Arthur* was written, MacLachlan was utterly surprised when her mother told her that the prism episode was drawn from a girlhood experience of MacLachlan's. At the time her mother pointed this out, MacLachlan insisted that she had made up the episode, but her mother was firm, "Oh no you didn't. . . . That happened."[3]

In the penultimate episode, Aunt Elda goes shopping, and Uncle Wrisby goes after Moreover to tell him that Pauline seems to be doing poorly. In the meantime, Arthur and Moira agree to stay with Pauline. They decide to give her some tonic as a curative, but not until they test it out themselves first. Before long they are both drunk on the highly potent medicine. Arthur and Moira parade to Moreover's house, tripping and giggling all the way, and when they arrive, they encounter the social worker there for her inspection visit. Moreover is mortified by the children's drunken condition. He immediately bends Moira over his knee and spanks her. Moira responds, between her tears, "Oh, Moreover, . . . you *do* love me!" (103). It was the outward, visible evidence that Moira had long been awaiting, although today, in our abuse-conscious society, some readers may look askance on Moreover's method of expressing his love. At any rate, the social worker is satisfied that Moreover is providing a suitable home for Moira. A delighted Moira writes a note to Arthur describing her elation: "Do you know what I feel like, Mouse? A baby. That's what. A baby starting out from the beginning. Thanks, Mouse" (105). It is impossible to overlook the symbolic reference to birthing, the imagery is so pervasive throughout the book. It is also significant that Moira, ever a person of action, chooses for once to adopt Arthur's medium: She *writes* to him, a sign of her own development of new perspectives. Arthur himself is finally encouraged to pen a brief note to his parents.

The final chapter brings the climax—a fierce thunderstorm, Aunt Elda and Uncle Wrisby going to town with Moreover, Moira staying with Arthur, and Arthur finally deciding to read the letters from home. The stage is set for Bernadette's birthing. When the children see the barn door open, they go out to investigate and find that Bernadette is missing. They find her in the mud with a seemingly lifeless baby pig beside her. Arthur immediately takes charge, and they erect a canvas over Bernadette and safely deliver her pigs under these extraordinary conditions. Even the runt of the litter is saved. Moira announces, "Arthur did it. . . . Arthur really *did* it all!" He is no longer Mouse, but his own agent, ready to assume his full identity as Moira calls him "Arthur for the very first time" (117).

Arthur, as MacLachlan's first venture into the novel, appropriately foreshadows many of the themes that will be her preoccupation in the novels to come. Cross-generational relationships, particularly that of parent and child, are examined in *Cassie Binegar* and later in *Sarah, Plain and Tall* and *Baby.* The cycle of life and the miracle of birth are central to *Unclaimed Treasures.* The conflict between fact and fiction and the meaning of each are a primary focus in *The Facts and Fictions of Minna Pratt.* The complexity of perspective and the necessity of seeing life from differing points of view are explored in *Journey.* The examination of art as a means of self-expression and of communication is found in every MacLachlan book in one form or another (just as in every book we find significant cross-generational relationships). And likewise pervasive is the conviction that all things are interdependent, that we all are tied to the great web of creation, that everyone and everything is somehow connected in wonderful and mysterious ways. *Arthur* is rich in intellectual seeds that would later develop into full-blown books of their own. Obviously, MacLachlan had a great deal to say, far more than could be accommodated in the simple tale of Arthur.

Some readers may find the book at times too precious— Arthur's pet mouse is a bit too cute, the characters too often slip into caricatures, the language is sometimes too clever, and the world of Aunt Elda and Uncle Wrisby's farm is a little too fanciful. But at the same time these are the very elements that keep a potentially dark and somber story lighthearted and comforting. MacLachlan deals with serious issues for a 10-year-old reader, and she rightly sets out to reassure as well as to entertain. Virginia Haviland noted that the "story may seem inconsequential" (while still pointing out that the "central interest is an engaging, very real child").[4] MacLachlan characteristically avoids the spectacular, finding instead the wonder in the everyday, the ordinary, the world in which most of us spend our lives. Her books are quiet and unassuming, but no less rich in their portrayal of the splendid tapestry of life.

Cassie Binegar

MacLachlan's second novel, *Cassie Binegar,* was published in 1982, the same year as her picture book *Mama One, Mama Two* and her fantasy *Tomorrow's Wizard.* On the surface, these appear to be very different books in both their format and subject matter. However, all three address the themes of accepting change, communicating feelings, and developing understanding.

In *Cassie Binegar,* MacLachlan picks up some of the threads from *Arthur, for the Very First Time* and weaves them into a new pattern. As one reviewer put it, "Every motif has its opposite number—for a story about waywardness and flux, this is highly patterned—and almost every moment is a rapt one."[5] The protagonist, Cassie Binegar ("whose name rhymes with vinegar"), is approximately the same age as Arthur Rasby, and like Arthur, she is having trouble with her family. As the book opens, we find Cassie writing in the sand on the beach, "I AM ANGRY." Like Arthur, Cassie aspires to be a writer; in fact, Cassie as a struggling artist is one of the dominant motifs of the story. She is angry about a lot of things. Her list currently numbers 22 complaints, including her family, her home, and her dry skin. The Binegars have only recently moved to the seaside where her father and brothers are fishermen and her mother manages some guest cottages. The Binegar household is loud, disorganized, unconventional, and loving. But Cassie wants, more than anything else, her own space. She is embarrassed by her family's raucous nature and wishes they could be more like her friend Margaret Mary's family—a prim and reserved English family living in a spotless, but unimaginative and dull, house. Cassie admires the plastic plants in Margaret Mary's house, "all perfect, every day the same" (39), sharply contrasting with her mother's wild and scattered garden.

On a visit to Margaret Mary's house, Cassie delights in the order and perfection, where everything is "nice." Margaret Mary, a girl wise beyond her years, notices Cassie's envy when she sees the matching hair ribbons hanging in the closet. They try unsuccessfully to tie up Cassie's hair in ribbons:

> "Cassie," said Margaret Mary, "your hair is splendid and free. It shouldn't be tied up in ribbons." Then, seeing Cassie's sad look she added, "They're only ribbons, Cass." She bent her head toward the closet. "They're only dresses. They're only socks" (21).

When Cassie notes that everything "is so neat and uncluttered . . . and safe," Margaret Mary remarks softly, "Only safe and uncluttered on the outside . . . This is all the outside. It doesn't matter. It only matters if you're safe and uncluttered on the inside" (22). We are reminded of the disheveled, sprawling house of Aunt Elda and Uncle Wrisby, and we will see a similar motif in *The Facts and Fictions of Minna Pratt.* The happily cluttered house seems to suggest that its occupants spend more time working on human relationships than on straightening and dusting.

Early in the story Cassie's relatives descend upon her household, beginning with her recently widowed grandmother, affectionately called "Gran." Cassie is dreading the arrival of Gran, whom she has not seen since her grandfather's death. In her heart, Cassie is carrying around a guilty secret, for the last time she spoke to her grandfather she shouted at him in anger; he demanded an apology, but she refused and stormed off. Shortly afterward, he died. Cassie blames herself and fears that Gran, a wise and perceptive woman, will guess Cassie's terrible secret—that she was responsible for her grandfather's death.

Cassie is wary of what to say to Gran and how to behave toward her now that she is a widow. It is the uneasiness many of us feel when first confronting the bereaved, almost as if we expect them to be entirely different people as a result of their loss. Her grandfather's death has greatly affected Cassie. She has even removed the grandfather doll from her dollhouse, wrapped it in tissue paper, and carefully placed it in her bureau drawer—a gesture, we later learn, of both reverence and guilt. Despite her mother's reassurances, Cassie does not relax until Gran actually arrives and proves to be as witty, wise, and caring as ever: "Gran was still Gran" (31). Of course, the lesson is that great changes will occur in our lives, and we will survive them; in many cases, we will be all the stronger for those changes. Cassie's mother acknowledges her daughter's dilemma: "Poor Cass, who wishes that things never changed" (43), and Gran takes it upon herself to help Cassie understand change and cope with it. Gran points out the hermit crab who must change shells as it grows: "He doesn't live in the same space all his life." But all Cassie can think is that she "wished most to be the hermit crab, happily carrying his space around with him" (37). The image of the hermit crab brings together two of the threads running through the book—Cassie's resistance to any kind of change and her fervent desire for a space of her own, a place where she can pursue her introspection privately.

Cassie's troubles seem to be following hard upon the heels of one another. As embarrassed as she is about her immediate family—her father, mother, and brothers—her eccentric extended family is almost too much for her to bear. Still more relatives arrive, including Uncle Hat, who relishes hats and has the peculiar habit of talking in rhyme; Cousin Coralinda, who is recently divorced and has a love of flamboyant clothing with too many feathers; and Baby Binnie, who steadfastly refuses to talk. In MacLachlan's work, eccentric behavior may be the sign of a self-confident, free spirit, or it may disguise an inner, psychological turmoil. In the case of these three relatives, the latter is true. Of course, the descent of the relatives promises to bring even more unwelcome changes to Cassie's turbulent life. One change, however, proves fortunate for Cassie, and that is the huge tablecloth that Coralinda gives Cassie's mother. The tablecloth drapes to the floor on all sides of the dining room table, providing Cassie with a hiding place, finally a space of her own.

It is here that Cassie is hiding when she meets Jason, a young writer who is renting one of her parents' cottages. Cassie has been listening to the conversation between Jason and her mother as they sit at the table. When the writer bends over and lifts the tablecloth to search for Bitsy, the missing cat, he finds himself eye-to-eye with Cassie. He earns her undying trust when he does not betray her secret. Almost immediately Cassie falls in love (or so she believes) with the writer. (The preadolescent girl falling in love with an older man is a concept MacLachlan will explore more fully in *Unclaimed Treasures*.)

Margaret Mary chides Cassie for her eavesdropping beneath the table, but Cassie justifies it as part of her preparation for becoming a writer. However, when she accidentally hears an emotional exchange between her mother and Coralinda, Cassie learns that some conversations are not to be overheard. She is pained by Coralinda's loneliness and unhappiness since her husband "flew the coop," as Gran says. It is also during one of Cassie's eavesdropping sessions under the table that Baby Binnie crawls beneath the draping tablecloth and plays a game of hide-and-seek with Cassie. Baby Binnie looks at Cassie and says, "Cass," her first recognizable word. Unfortunately, only Cassie hears her, and she cannot report the gleeful news without revealing her clandestine activities.

Shortly after, when she finally has a conversation with Jason the writer, he admonishes her for hiding. She explains that she hides because "hiding is the best way to find what you want to know." But Jason disagrees, "Not so, . . . Being a part of it all is the best way" (67). This, of course, sounds very much like Moira's advice to Arthur. Jason suggests that asking questions might be a better way of learning about things than eavesdropping, and further recommends that Cassie write out her questions. So she places a sheet of paper on the bathroom wall and makes two columns, one for questions and one for answers. Then she poses her own question: "Why don't I have a space of my own?" (69). Jason writes the answer: "Each of us has a space of his own. We carry it around as close as skin, as private as our dreams. What makes you think you don't have your own, too?" (73). Cassie resents her question being answered with another question.

Soon a relationship begins to develop between Jason and Coralinda, and Jason is particularly fond of Baby Binnie. While taking tea with Jason, Cassie finds a cup filled with feathers, obviously fallen from Coralinda's fantastic garments. Cassie snips that "she must be shedding," and Jason corrects her, "Molting, I think the word is. . . . Actually, I would prefer to call it emerging" (77). This leads to talk of change, the dominant image being the butterfly emerging from its cocoon, and Jason notes that "sometimes we build cocoons around us and linger inside awhile" (78). Cassie recalls the earlier conversation between her mother and Coralinda, the one she overheard while beneath the table, in which her mother remarked that Coralinda wore feathers for very much the same reason that Uncle Hat wore hats and spoke in rhymes—they are all ways of spinning cocoons about us and hiding from reality. The disparate images slowly converge to form a pattern that Cassie only gradually comprehends: "Why is it . . . that I like to hear what you say even though I don't understand what you're saying at all?" she asks the bemused Jason (79).

Another image, in addition to the hermit crab and the cocoon, that dramatizes the element of change in our lives comes from Margaret Mary. She delights in the time she spends with Cassie's family; she appreciates their liveliness, their openly expressed love for each other. She asks Cassie's father and brothers what it is like to fish on the sea. They describe the storms, the calm, the power, and Cassie's father finally says, "It is somehow always the same and yet never the same . . . but always beautiful." And Margaret Mary exclaims, "Like a kaleidoscope!" (43), another symbol of life's inevitable changes. Margaret Mary recalls:

> "When I was very little, in England, I had one. I would turn it and turn it and the pieces of glass would fall into patterns, all lovely. But I would want one pattern—one special one—to stay there forever. But the pieces of glass would fall into another shape, then another. And they were never the same."
>
> "But always beautiful," said Cassie's mother softly.
>
> "I remember," said Cassie. "I always wanted one to stay the same for always."
>
> "And you still do," said Gran. (43)

Gran later expands on this theme when, just as she is about to begin painting a picture, she explains to Cassie about different perspectives: "It's as if we all have eyeglasses to look through—eyeglasses of our own"; however, she points out that growing up means that we must learn "how to look through other people's eyeglasses" (84–85). And then she horrifies Cassie when she tells her that Cassie's beloved grandfather, whom Cassie called "Papa," never learned to do that. "But Papa was perfect!" Cassie protests. Gently Gran reminds her of a time when Cassie grew furious because the snowflakes she caught on her mitten could not be preserved in their perfection. Gran points out that Papa was very much like that. "He never learned that most things are only there for a moment, quite perfect and fine, like snow" (86). Catching snow becomes for Cassie another image of the inevitability of change. With this newfound insight, she goes about asking people how they feel about catching snow. She is surprised when Uncle Hat replies to her in prose and not in his customary rhyme. When she remarks on the phenomenon, he simply replies, "Sometimes I don't have to. . . . Everyone has his own way of hiding, Cassie. Twelve and two / The same with you" (92). Her questioning has brought Cassie to some important conclusions: "Looking through the eyeglasses of others, thought Cassie. She thought of her father, running from a taxi through the crowds to buy violets [for Cassie's mother who gave birth to her in a taxi]. She thought of Uncle Hat, sometimes rhyming, sometimes not. Coralinda wearing feathers, but changing before her eyes, becoming beautiful" (93). A turning point then comes when Cassie notes some real flowers, marigolds, growing in Margaret Mary's lawn. When Cassie asks why they are there, Margaret Mary replies: "Well, . . . they grow, for one thing. They'll grow and fill in all the spaces here. And they'll change. New blooms. They won't always look the same" (94). To that Cassie gives a resounding, "Splendid . . . That's splendid." The images are all falling into a clear pattern now.

The book is largely composed of a series of quiet vignettes, but dramatic tension occurs toward the end when Cassie's father and brothers are at sea during a storm. Cassie notices for the first time the small lines of worry around her mother's mouth and on her forehead. When Cassie remarks that she never knew her mother worried because "it doesn't show," her mother replies, "I guess,

Cass, that's because you can't see what goes on inside my head. . . . It's private." Suddenly Cassie realizes "I do have my own space" (99). She pencils these words onto the sheet in the bathroom and draws beneath the words a pair of eyeglasses, a symbol of her enlightened vision. She then goes to the attic to look for a kaleidoscope, where she finds Gran searching for her lavender wedding dress, which was also Cassie's mother's wedding dress. This dress becomes a symbol of the circle of life, for Gran intends that Cassie will wear the dress at her own wedding, and weddings also signify change.

Meanwhile, outside, the storm has become fierce. Everyone begins to grow anxious for Cassie's father and brothers. In her anxiety Cassie tearfully confesses to Gran the tremendous guilt she has harbored ever since her grandfather's death. A surprised Gran firmly tells Cassie the facts about her grandfather's death: that he was very sick, and that he, too, yelled before he died. "He sat up," Gran says, "and yelled 'Where in hell are my green socks!' Then he died. That was all" (107). Gran tells Cassie how she herself faced her grief:

> "You know, after Papa died I came on a footprint of his in the garden. It was so perfect, so clear, just as if he'd passed that way a moment before. I would go out and look at it, day after day. Once I even put a wooden carton over it so it would stay. But it didn't. The rain began to wash it away, slowly, and one day it wasn't there anymore."
> There was silence.
> "Like catching snow," said Cassie in Gran's ear. (107)

They then notice that the storm has subsided, dramatically symbolizing Cassie's assuaged grief.

In the final chapter, Gran unveils the painting that she has been working on for Cassie. It is of Cassie in the lavender wedding dress, painted by Gran because "I may never get to see you at your own wedding, you know." In a gesture that at once signifies Cassie's unselfishness and her acceptance of the inevitability of change, she gives the portrait back to Gran: "I think you should have it. For a while, at least. Later it can be mine" (114). The chapter is filled with symbolic gestures: Baby Binnie decides to speak publicly for the first time, to the family's great relief. Another silence broken. Later that night, Cassie dreams of the hermit crab—a dual symbol, carrying its own space with it and, when it grows, moving on to a new space, accepting the inevitable change. Cassie awakens and replaces the grandfather doll in her dollhouse: "It's the same as being here" (116). Then she opens her notebook and completes her poem, "Spaces," identifying her favorite space as "Behind my nose, / Behind my face . . . Where I sort out my thoughts and sighs and shouts! and cries" (114). She then crosses out "THE END" and writes "THE BEGINNING."

The book closes with a newspaper announcement of the wedding of Coralinda and Jason. We are informed that, at the wedding, Cassie wore the heirloom lavender dress and read a poem of her own composition. MacLachlan here weaves together the various motifs of the story, although some readers may find the passage a bit too contrived: The couple is married on "Snow Shore" at sunrise, and we learn that Jason's first short story, "Catching Snow," is about to be published. The flowers—real, of course—are provided by Margaret Mary. No loose end is left untied. And so this story about changes ends with still another change for the family—a wedding—and it is a change that Cassie readily accepts, a sign of her psychological growth.

Not to be overlooked are the many references to art throughout the book. Cassie's mother plays the flute (MacLachlan never omits the music). Gran paints, Jason is a writer, Uncle Hat is a poet of sorts, and Cassie is an aspiring writer. It is through their art that these characters are able to fully express themselves, and it is through art that they come to understand others (Cassie realizes a great deal about her own place in the cycle of life when she sees Gran's portrait of her in the family wedding dress). For MacLachlan, art is communication on a deeper level (or higher plane); it is wisdom and delight.

In the dedication to *The Facts and Fictions of Minna Pratt,* MacLachlan acknowledges her debt to Natalie Babbitt. In *Tuck*

Everlasting, Babbitt emphasizes the necessity of change in the face of our natural antipathy to it. The Tuck family is removed from the cycle of life because of their accidentally acquired immortality, which they find to be no boon. Angus Tuck says:

> Everything's a wheel, turning and turning, never stopping. The frogs is part of it, and the bugs, and the fish, and the wood thrush, too. And people. But never the same ones. Always coming in new, always growing and changing, and always moving on. That's the way it's supposed to be. That's the way it *is.* . . . Dying's part of the wheel, right there next to being born. You can't pick out the pieces you like and leave the rest. Being part of the whole thing, that's the blessing.[6]

Unclaimed Treasures

The theme of life's cyclical nature is the central focus of *Unclaimed Treasures* (1984), MacLachlan's third novel for intermediate readers. Here MacLachlan surrenders more completely to her fascination with art in its various forms, including painting, music, and creative writing. For MacLachlan, art is an integral part of life, and this conviction is evident in everything she writes.

Unclaimed Treasures is an unusual book for youthful readers, both in its theme and its structure. It is, in fact, a love story (even more so than was *Cassie Binegar*)—a literary form uncommon in books for middle-aged children. And it is a story of embedded narratives—a story within a story within a story. The framing story is set in the present and consists of a pregnant woman and her husband reminiscing about their first meeting when they were both "nearly twelve." This reminiscence—the summer adventures of Willa Pinkerton, her twin brother Nicholas, and their new neighbor, Horace Morris—constitutes the principal embedded narrative. It is a novel that is designed to be self-consciously a work of literary art—its three parts are titled "Beginning," "Middle," and "End"—undoubtedly MacLachlan's overture to her fourth-grade teacher who instructed her to write a story with these distinctive elements.

Willa and Nicholas's father is a college creative-writing professor, and their mother is expecting her third child, a fact causing
some embarrassment for Willa who thinks her mother much too
old for that sort of thing. Horace Morris and his father, Matthew,
an artist, have moved in with two spinster aunts (affectionately
called the "Unclaimed Treasures") next door to the Pinkertons.
Horace's mother has temporarily left the family to do some soul-
searching. (The separation of parents and children has always held
a special interest for MacLachlan.) When the story opens, Willa
and Nicholas are invited next door to a wake for a third aunt, who
has just died. They are surprised to witness such a joyous occasion—loud chatter, much eating and drinking, not to mention a
cat preening in the coffin with the deceased. The funeral is a deliberate artifice designed to underscore one of MacLachlan's most
salient themes—birth, life, and death all wrapped together into
an ever continuing cycle, without beginning, middle, or end. The
aunt's death is also a separation, and the coping with loss on a
variety of planes is another theme of the novel. The story, in fact,
begins with a death and ends with a birth, an inversion of the way
we normally consider the cycle of life. The surviving aunts, the
"Unclaimed Treasures," are characters reminiscent of MacLachlan's elderly people elsewhere—dressed in bright colors, outspoken, and carefree, the essence of life.

Willa, on the verge of pubescence, confesses to Nicholas that
she is in love with Horace's father, whom she believes to be available since his wife has abandoned her family "to seek her fortune."
Nicholas, one of a series of MacLachlan's sage and understanding
siblings, warns that she will be hurt, but Willa tries to ignore him
(although she "knew now and had always known that Nicky was
wiser" [17]). In the process of cleaning her father's study, Willa
discovers a student's writing assignment, a sentimental and melo-
dramatic love story about Ted and Wanda that seems to capture
perfectly Willa's adolescent emotional state. The narrative occasionally returns to vapid passages from Ted and Wanda's story,
which serves as commentaries on Willa's one-sided affair with
Matthew. The "story" of Ted and Wanda is not really a story at all.

It has no plot and consists largely of Wanda and Ted ogling each
other and exchanging puerile sentiments:

> "Ted, Ted, sweet Ted," murmured Wanda. "Come and regard
> the sunrise."
> "Wonderful Wanda," exclaimed Ted in wonderful wonderment.
> "Let me see you when the light is best." (39)

The student's fatuous composition keeps the reader appropriately
distanced from Willa's imagined love affair with Matthew. The
Ted and Wanda passages also underscore the absurdity of Willa's
(as well as Wanda's) schoolgirl crush—a fact that Willa will eventually come to appreciate.

We are introduced to yet one more set of minor characters:
Porky Atwater, a neighbor; his great-grandfather, appropriately
named "Old Pepper," for he is spry and wily; and their pet parrot,
Bella-Marie. Old Pepper is another in MacLachlan's gallery of
ancient eccentrics. When we first meet them, Porky is pushing
Old Pepper in a wheelbarrow, and they are searching for the parrot. Old Pepper is described as a "dried apple of a man—nearly
one or two hundred years old" (21); he frequently forgets to wear
his teeth and occasionally forgets to wear his clothes—"though
[we are assured] he never wanders naked from his own backyard."
Horace notes that he looks "Innocent, like a naked baby at the
beach" (22), a reference that eventually takes on added meaning
as the themes of dying and new life are interwoven. Old Pepper
and the "Unclaimed Treasures" could be viewed as constant
reminders of our mortality, of endings. But in their exuberance
and their delightful eccentricity, we see only an affirmation of life.

In addition to pursuing her love interest in Matthew, Willa is
obsessed with wanting to do something important, something
extraordinary—yet she finds it difficult to determine just what is
ordinary and what is extraordinary. She has harbored an admira-
tion for Horace's mother for having the courage to go off on her
own to pursue her dreams. Willa is dismayed to learn that her
own mother gave up a promising career in dancing to have children. It is a sacrifice beyond Willa's comprehension, and she

insists that her mother should have stayed with the dancing, that "it's important." But her mother points out that "there are different kinds of important" (29–30). Willa is not only angry with her mother for giving up her chance to do something extraordinary with her dance but also for settling for a lackluster lifestyle and for being pregnant.

Her frustration with her mother builds upon the little things. When Horace and his father come to dinner, Willa is horrified that her mother would serve something as uninspired as chicken pot pie. During this dinner party, Matthew admires Nicholas's artwork, particularly a drawing of a newly planted garden with long furrows and a fenced border. It is a favorite of both Nicholas and Willa, although their mother wonders where the rest of the garden is. Whether their mother is genuinely puzzled or whether she is joking is not something that Willa bothers to discover. With the impatience of youth, Willa becomes inwardly infuriated at what she perceives to be her mother's lack of imagination. Willa thinks indignantly to herself, but does not say to her brother, "Why don't you tell her the garden is there, just beneath the surface, about to come up?" (36). Of course, the garden not yet come to fruition is like their pregnant mother—but that is not a connection that Willa herself can make yet. Willa, who is not an artist (making her unusual among MacLachlan's protagonists, who typically pursue some form of art), is invited to become part of an artistic endeavor when Matthew asks her to sit for him so that he might complete a portrait. In fact, it is a portrait originally modeled by Winnie, Matthew's wife. Willa is ecstatic—her "true love" has actually asked her to take the place of his absent wife. This concludes the first part of the tale—"The Beginning."

At this point the reader returns to the framing story and begins to realize that the woman speaking is Willa, although no names are used. The couple's thoughts turn to Old Pepper and his comment that "things are seldom as they seem. You must do better than just look" (ironically recalling Willa's exasperation with her mother's failure to look deeply enough at Nicholas's drawing). He also told them that "it was everyday things that matter" (43). MacLachlan never tires of bringing this point home. Her attention to the simple, quiet affairs of everyday life is found throughout her writing. Young Willa's immaturity clouds her judgment, and she fails to see the importance of the "everyday things." Of course, much of Willa's problem is egocentrism, her inability to see other points of view—a very natural childhood malady and one commonly found among MacLachlan's heroes and heroines. (A similar problem plagues both Arthur and Cassie Binegar, as well as virtually every other child who is "nearly twelve.")

In the second part of the principal narrative, entitled simply "The Middle," we see the beginning of Willa's transformation as she gingerly puts herself in the shoes of others. She and Horace listen to Horace's aunts practicing a Beethoven trio—Aunt Crystal used to be a noted violist and Aunt Lulu plays the flute (this book is filled with artists). But they are missing the third member, who Horace tells Willa was his mother, a violinist. "They miss her," he says. But at that point, "Willa's heart moved, a sudden wrenching feeling that was new to her" (52). What Willa realizes is that it is Horace who misses his mother; she notices the sadness and the longing in his eyes. She does not yet realize her own selfish motive in wanting Winnie absent (that is, to clear the way to her true love, Matthew). As in real life, wisdom is most often acquired gradually with quiet and unassuming revelations, not suddenly with loud and flashing thunderbolts.

When Willa accompanies her mother to the obstetrician's office, she finds herself full of pity for the pregnant women there. She is particularly piqued by the doctor's secretary—"tall and thin, like a praying mantis . . . Willa thought it was bad taste, or at least unkind, for the doctor to hire such a girl to sit in front of all the fat women" (53). These sentiments seem more characteristic of an adult than of 12-year-old Willa, particularly when she prays to God to "make the beautiful skinny secretary as fat and swollen as the rest. Make her have varicose veins; make her shift and sigh. Uncurl her hair, God. Amen and over" (54). It is in the doctor's office that Willa first sees the movements of the baby in her mother's abdomen. Later that evening Willa is shown a sonogram of the baby, taken in the doctor's office as a precaution against the risks of the pregnancy. Willa looks carefully at her mother and observes her tears of happiness and apprehension. For the first time Willa realizes that the baby is a live human being, that it is real, just like her. This is Willa's second awakening.

When Willa sits for Matthew, she wears a lacy white dress that makes her look tall and stately, but she feels wrong, wrong because the girl she sees in the mirror is not Willa Pinkerton. She is beginning to feel the sadness that Nicholas predicted when she told him that Matthew was her "true love." Her racing emotions stir up confusion in her mind—she thinks of her unrequited love for Matthew, of the moving baby inside her mother, of the figure in the painting, of the girl in the mirror. The images move rapidly across Willa's mind. That evening Willa's mother comforts her, reassuring her that the baby will be fine and reminiscing about Willa and Nicholas's births and how she was glad to give up her dancing for the sake of her children. Willa is finally ready to accept this change in her life and even asks if she can help care for the new baby. When the sonogram reveals that the baby is a girl, Willa is "nearly overcome with joy." She announces to Nicholas, "We've got us a sister!" (67).

But the discussion of the impending birth is quickly followed by a discussion between the children and Old Pepper about death. Old Pepper speaks quite matter-of-factly about his own death: "It is, after all, my life. I don't mind" (72). MacLachlan, in her books, is too absorbed with the affirmation of life to spend a great deal of time pondering death. But neither is death ignored or put aside. Rather, it is depicted as a natural consequence of life, as just one more part of living. Death is neither mournful nor lugubrious. The rather gay wake with which the book opens at the home of the "Unclaimed Treasures," Old Pepper's musing about his own approaching death (he expects to die before his parrot), and Nicholas's surprising announcement that he wishes to be buried standing up ("I hate to lie down")—all these references suggest not so much a flippancy as a matter-of-factness about the prospect of death.

The final interlude, prior to the third part, "The End," presents us with more hints as to the identity of the man and woman, although there is little doubt now about Willa's identity. She prepares us for the final act by commenting on a torn piece of paper with the letters "ILLA" printed on it: *"That . . . has to do with something very extraordinary I did once upon a summer when there was a tree full of blooms that would become apples, and a pair of twins, a boy and a girl"* (81).

In fact, Willa does two extraordinary things. First, she meets Wanda, her father's student, the author of the insipid manuscript that has been such a preoccupation of Willa's. It is only now that Willa discovers that "Ted" is her father (she quite naturally had never made the connection before; 12-year-olds seldom think of their parents as having first names). Furthermore, Wanda shows up at Willa's house with a picnic basket, hoping to entice her professor to amble down by some "gentle stream" where they can discuss her writing. Significantly, when Wanda meets Willa, Willa is standing on her head in her father's study in order to get more blood to her brain. Roberta Seelinger Trites points out that "Willa's position helps her to gain a different perspective on the events around her, just as the binoculars help Arthur change his subject position in *Arthur, for the Very First Time.*"[7] On another level perhaps, Willa's perception of Wanda from upside down dramatizes the absurdity of Wanda and her empty writing and helps bring Willa toward a more mature understanding of her life.

In a wonderfully comic moment, Willa decides to take advantage of the fact that Wanda is obviously ignorant of Professor Pinkerton's family. Willa fabricates a story about the professor's children (more than a dozen) and the impending birth of his grandchild. The ruse sufficiently scares off the young coed, and the whole family enjoys a good laugh when Willa recounts the incident. Nicholas is amazed by the entire thing, for he never once suspected that the writer of the syrupy prose had a crush on his father. "How did you know?" he asks Willa. "I knew Wanda well," is her simple reply (88). In Wanda, Willa sees herself and realizes that her relationship with Matthew is just as one-sided as was Wanda's with her father. This gives her the wisdom and the courage to take the next extraordinary step of the summer.

Willa completes her sitting for Matthew and decides to leave him a note reading: "Matthew, I'll love you forever. WILLA."

But when she goes to deliver the note, she discovers a strange woman in Matthew's studio. Willa asks her if she is "another Unclaimed Treasure," to which the woman responds, "I suppose I am. We are all, let us hope, unclaimed treasures" (92). Almost instinctively, they know each other. It is, of course, Matthew's wife, Winnie. For Willa it is an epiphany, just as when she saw the sonogram of her baby sister: *"Winnie is real."* But more signif-icantly, she realizes that Winnie loves Matthew and that Matthew loves her. After Winnie leaves, Willa examines the fin-ished portrait and notices in one corner the words, "Portrait of W." This gives her the idea to carefully tear the "ILLA" from her note and prop the remainder up against the portrait. She had intended to do something extraordinary today—professing her love openly for Matthew. Indeed, in her unselfish act, she does do something extraordinary and manages to bring Matthew and Winnie back together. Willa may seem, to many adult readers at least, wise far beyond her years. But she remains a consistent character, true to her precocious nature, observant, introspective, ever learning and growing.

When Horace reveals to Willa that he knows she left the note that achieved his parents' reunion, his gratitude results in Willa's first real kiss—"lots better than a mahogany bedpost [where she had practiced her kissing technique]. A warm pair of human lips . . . Extraordinary" (99). The final two chapters constitute the only real action in the story. Horace, Nicholas, and Willa discover a fire in Matthew's attic studio. Nicholas climbs a tree to rescue the painting, and falls in the process. The excitement brings on his mother's labor, and the two of them are rushed to the hospital in an ambulance. Old Pepper insists on driving Willa and Horace to the hospital in Willa's father's car, but he knows nothing about the foot pedals, so Horace works the pedals for him while Old Pepper sits "happily steering and making wild hand signals out the window" (108). All turns out well, Nicholas recovers, the new baby, Jane, arrives, and Willa realizes as she gazes about the room with Horace, Nicholas, and her new sister that they are all "Unclaimed Treasures"—that each individual is extraordinary and just waiting to be discovered. Her search is over.

It is Horace who suggests that the baby be named Jane—
"straightforward and honest and calm" (91). The family's adopt-
ing of Horace's suggestion, Trites says, affirms "both his agency
and his interconnectedness with other people."[8] This interconnectedness takes on added meaning when we learn that Horace
eventually marries Willa and becomes Jane's brother-in-law.

The book closes with the framing story functioning as a sort of
epilogue. The man and woman are identified as Willa and
Nicholas, and we learn that Willa and Horace are expecting a
baby. The conclusion seems designed for those readers who are
anxious to know what happens after the story's ending. If this
conclusion seems a bit too tidy (Matthew and Winnie are off seeking their fortunes, Willa's mother is at last pursuing her dancing,
and Nicholas has his own studio), we need not fret too much over
it. The point is not that things turn out well but that things keep
moving; life is not static—life does not end as a story does, but
keeps on going. Trites notes that "the cyclical structure that
MacLachlan employs [in *Unclaimed Treasures*] emphasizes narrative
(and its function as a metaphorical representation of life) as something that simply includes closure as a normal function of narrative (and life) rather than privileging closure as the most important aspect of narrative (and life)."[9]

It is interesting how frequently pregnancy figures into
MacLachlan's work, and it usually signifies the cyclical nature of
life, continuity amidst change. Willa's reaction is typical of many
MacLachlan protagonists; she not only rejects her mother's pregnancy (like Arthur, she tries to ignore it) but also dismisses having
babies as something neither important nor extraordinary. Only
with her maturing does she realize the power and mystery of
birth. Both the framed and the framing narrative climax in the
births of babies—Willa's sister, Jane, in the former and Willa's
own baby in the latter. It is Nicholas who gives the last significant
speech in the book when, just as he is about to leave for the hospital with the expectant Willa, he tells his baby sister Jane, *"I'll come
back later and tell you a story about extraordinary things. A story with a
beginning and a middle. And an end that begins another story"* (118).
And the cycle begins again.

Willa, like both Arthur and Cassie Binegar, are initially observers of life rather than participants in life. All three characters have to learn to join in the process of living. Willa, although she is not an artist, is surrounded by art and profoundly affected by it. It is interesting that the art described in the book is all somehow incomplete: Matthew's portrait of Winnie is yet to be finished, the "Unclaimed Treasures" attempt the Beethoven trio without the third musician, and the short story of Wanda and Ted is itself only a fragment. All of this incomplete art mirrors Willa's incomplete self, but more importantly, it is Willa who enables the completion of all these artistic endeavors. She poses for the portrait so that it might be finished, she engineers Winnie and Matthew's reunion, and she mercifully brings an end to the Wanda and Ted saga. But Willa is not only about endings; she is about beginnings as well, and her impending childbirth in the framing story closes the book with a new beginning. *Unclaimed Treasures* is a more self-consciously artful book than its predecessors, its contrapuntal narrative design adding richness to the predominant themes. With its hint of mystery, its delightful cast of characters, and its highly sensitive treatment of issues confronting the typical "nearly 12-year-old," *Unclaimed Treasures* demonstrates MacLachlan's increasing mastery of her art, which will be rewarded in her next achievement, the Newbery Medal–winning *Sarah, Plain and Tall*.

Chapter Four

Journey to the Past:
Sarah, Plain and Tall and *Skylark*

There is always something to miss, no matter where you are.
—*Sarah, Plain and Tall*

When *Sarah, Plain and Tall* won the 1986 Newbery Medal, the name of Patricia MacLachlan achieved the celebrity status that typically comes with that recognition. Although the Newbery Medal honors a single book, her three novels preceding *Sarah, Plain and Tall* also deserve to bathe in some of the glory. However, in some respects, *Sarah, Plain and Tall* represents a departure from MacLachlan's previous novels, specifically in its historical setting, its first-person narrative, and its more serious theme. All these are features that will become part of MacLachlan's subsequent novels. So it is in several ways that *Sarah, Plain and Tall* marks a turning point in MacLachlan's career. The following discussion treats both *Sarah, Plain and Tall* and its sequel, *Skylark*, although the latter did not appear in print until some nine years after *Sarah*. The convenience of discussing these closely related works in a single chapter seemed to outweigh the temptation to follow MacLachlan's career with absolute chronology.

Sarah, Plain and Tall

Patricia MacLachlan has always felt deeply rooted in the past and strongly influenced by family and "the familiar ebb and flow of daily life."[1] But it is in *Sarah, Plain and Tall* that she surrenders most completely to her attachments, which undoubtedly accounts for the passion so evident in the story's telling. *Sarah, Plain and Tall* is MacLachlan's most celebrated book, not only winning the 1986 Newbery Medal but achieving even wider fame as a Hallmark Hall of Fame television play. In this book and in *Skylark*, MacLachlan returns to the briefer format she used in *Tomorrow's*

Wizard and *Seven Kisses in a Row. Sarah, Plain and Tall* and *Skylark,* however, are written as cohesive novellas and are addressed to a somewhat older audience than those earlier works—readers of about 8 to 10 years of age.

Sarah, Plain and Tall is indeed a very personal story for MacLachlan. The germ for *Sarah* was one she carried around for many years, originating with a story her mother told her about one of their ancestors who acquired a mail-order bride. MacLachlan first used the idea in *Arthur, for the Very First Time* when Aunt Elda reminisces about her childhood. In that story, the mail-order bride is Aunt Elda's stepmother, Aunt Mag. Aunt Elda's mother died while giving birth to Aunt Elda, and she was cared for by her older sisters until she was four. At that time, her father, whose name is Caleb, writes a newspaper ad for help. "For a house-keeper?" Arthur asks. "No, . . . For a wife," Aunt Elda replies, with words repeated almost verbatim in *Sarah, Plain and Tall.* The ad is answered by a "strong-faced woman with steady eyes" from the Maine seacoast. The children like her immediately, despite her gruffness and imposing appearance, "raw-boned and tall." Aunt Mag, as the children call her, is a warm and sensitive woman who provides much-needed stability for the family. She is also a very wise woman who knows the importance of the past and of the children's connection to their own mother. She shares a prism with them, and as it casts its light about the room she tells them, "You won't remember your mother . . . but you will learn that her life touches yours. All of us touch each other. Just like the colors of the prism. Don't you forget that." Aunt Mag tells them stories, leaves her hair out for the birds to use in their nests, plows the field, and wins an enduring place in the hearts of all the family members.

Instinctively, MacLachlan knew that the character of Aunt Mag was simply too rich with possibilities to be left to languish in a brief reminiscence. She was a character that haunted, nagged, or begged MacLachlan to tell her story. But MacLachlan had yet another, sadder motivation for telling the story. Her mother had been diagnosed with Alzheimer's disease and the family was com-pelled to watch her memory fade. MacLachlan wished to preserve

Sarah as a piece of her mother's past, not only for her mother but for herself and her children. We are often told by the best children's writers that they do not write for children, but for themselves, and this seems to be especially true of MacLachlan in *Sarah, Plain and Tall.*

And so MacLachlan takes the character of Aunt Mag and transforms her into Sarah Wheaton, also of the Maine seacoast and also plain and tall. The name of Caleb is resurrected, but now it is given to a boy, the younger of the two children of Jacob Witting, a poor farmer on the broad prairie. (We are never told the exact time or place of the novel's setting, although the movie sets the story in 1910—we might have guessed much earlier from the text.) The older child is Anna, who is about 10 and has cared for her younger brother since her mother died while giving birth to him about five years before. The story opens with Caleb plying Anna with questions about their mother: "Did she sing every day? . . . Every single day? . . . And did Papa sing, too? . . . What did I look like when I was born?" (*Sarah,* 3–4). Caleb asks for the oft-told story about his own birth and his mother's death. Anna is clearly irritated at having to repeat it for "the hundredth time this year," but she does so. Caleb begs her to remember some of Mama's songs: "Maybe . . . if you remember the songs, then I might remember her, too" (*Sarah,* 6). It is a book very much about memories, of summoning up past joys, not to help us escape from present sorrows but to help us remember how to celebrate, to hope, to love. Caleb's request reminds us of the importance of storytelling in keeping our past alive, in maintaining those connections with our roots, in establishing our identities. Of course, the past contains not only joy but also pain and regret. Anna, the narrator of the story, relates her own guilt—she had forgotten to say good night to her mother the night before her death, and she is plagued with remorse, suffering in much the same way as Cassie Binegar suffers for her display of anger just before her grandfather's death. Anna also recalls how long it took her to love Caleb, for she blamed him for her mother's death. In a brief scene and with very few words, MacLachlan is able to convey a variety of complex emotions surrounding the loss of a parent.

Papa is a quiet, diffident man who uses the idea of memory to broach the subject of the mail-order bride. When Caleb notes that his father does not sing anymore, Papa says it is because "I've forgotten the old songs. . . . But maybe there's a way to remember them" (*Sarah*, 7). He has advertised for a wife and has in hand the reply from Sarah Wheaton. Her letter is frank and straightforward: "I am not mild mannered," she advises (*Sarah*, 9). Both Anna and Caleb seem delighted with the prospect of a new mother. Anna asks only one thing: "Ask her if she sings" (*Sarah*, 10). A charming exchange of letters is then recounted, in which Sarah writes to each of the children detailing her background. Particularly evident is her love of the sea; her favorite colors are the colors of the sea—blue and green and gray. Sarah's attachment to the sea is a cause of great concern for the children, who fear she will not like the prairie, its landscape contrasting so markedly. Caleb is most anxious for Sarah's arrival; Anna is more reserved, not from any perceived jealousy or reluctance over having someone take her mother's place but simply because she has learned to live with loss and disappointment and is more guarded with her feelings. (Anna's character undergoes a significant change in the screenplay, which will be discussed later.) In a postscript to her final letter to their father before her arrival on the prairie, Sarah writes simply, "Tell them I sing" (*Sarah*, 15). MacLachlan resists all temptation to elaborate on the comment. She permits it to stand by itself. Her style is terse, but evocative, and with the careful use of words and imagery, she conveys a depth of feeling and thoughtfulness in her characters that is seldom found in works of this brevity. Here MacLachlan has perfected the style of understatement and has learned the proverbial wisdom of the old Chinese painter who, when asked what the most important part of his painting was, replied, "The part that is left out."

Consequently, we do well to consider carefully every image, every reference, for the meaning it might hold. Sarah arrives with the spring, and this is very much a book of springtime, a book of new beginnings, of life starting afresh. She arrives with her cat named Seal, a seashell for Caleb, and a stone worn smooth by the sea for Anna, all emblems of her attachment to the sea. The children know instinctively that Sarah already misses the sea. Caleb listens carefully to Sarah's every word, clinging to those expressions that suggest that she might decide to stay with them permanently. He is thrilled when Sarah sets out to pick flowers to dry so they "can have flowers all winter." Caleb picks up immediately on her comments and whispers to Anna: "Sarah said winter. . . . That means Sarah will stay" (*Sarah,* 23).

Sarah's arrival in spring is fitting because in many important ways she is portrayed as a sort of earth mother. "The dogs loved Sarah first," Anna tells us (*Sarah,* 22). And so the animals, with their unfailing instinct, are the first ones to give Sarah their approval. And the animals' affection is merited, for Sarah is a woman of great compassion for all living things. She leaves the clippings from Caleb's haircut scattered about so the birds can gather it for their nests—just as Aunt Elda did in *Arthur, for the Very First Time.* Sarah loves the sheep and the cows and the chickens. She names the chickens and allows them into the house, and Anna observes, "I was right. The chickens would not be for eating" (*Sarah,* 43). And when she sings, Sarah sings of nature, of summer, and of birds: "Sumer is icumen in, / Lhude sing cuccu!" And a meadowlark joins her. These are all signs that Sarah, who was so much a part of the Maine seascape, is equally in tune with the rolling prairie.

Each chapter after Sarah's arrival begins with a reference to nature—the springtime and its blooming fields, the dogs that loved her first, the sheep that made her smile, the dandelions with "their heads as soft as feathers," the summer roses, the clouds, the rain, and the still air. The association of Sarah with nature and natural phenomena underscores her genuine, earthy character and may also suggest that her role in the Witting household is itself part of the natural cycle of things.

MacLachlan notes that one of the surprises for her while writing the book was her realization that the prairie and the sea had so much in common—particularly in color and space. This similarity is made clearer to the children when Sarah describes the dunes on the Maine coast. ("Dune" was, she tells us, her first word as a child.) Characteristically, Caleb is worried because they have no dunes on the prairie, but Papa comes to the rescue, pointing out that the haystack, "nearly half as tall as the barn," is like a dune. They take turns sliding down the dune, and when Sarah later refers to it as "our dune," Caleb secretly rejoices. Caleb embodies the hopefulness of the very young, and although we know that this innocence cannot last forever, we should be heartened that the cyclical nature of life will ensure the constant renewal of this joyous optimism. After having brought Maine to the children in the form of the "dune," Sarah teaches them to swim in the cow pond, the closest thing they have to the sea. Sarah is described again as an earth mother: serene, with cows watching on in wonder, "their eyes sad in their dinner-plate faces," with crows flying overhead, and a killdeer singing in a nearby field. Anna is convinced that "Sarah was happy" (*Sarah*, 37).

The only other characters in the book are the neighbors, Matthew and Maggie (herself a mail-order bride) and their two children, Rose and Violet. Maggie realizes that Sarah is lonely, and the two women confide in each other that they do, indeed, miss their homes. Maggie misses the hills of Tennessee and Sarah misses the sea and her brother and aunts. But Maggie points out, "There are always things to miss . . . No matter where you are" (*Sarah*, 40). And Anna herself recognizes that she would miss her dog, Nick; and of course, she misses her own mother. She is close to realizing that it is the very fact that Sarah does miss Maine, the sea, and her family that makes her so special to Anna and Caleb. Her warmth and sensitivity, her fondness of the landscape, her devotion to nature—just as these qualities threaten to pull her back to Maine, they also make it possible for her to stay on the prairie. Maggie brings Sarah plants for a garden, a fitting gift of welcome, but Sarah's acceptance of the gift is also a sign of her determination to stay to see the garden flourish. When Matthew extends his welcome to Sarah, he explains that "Maggie misses her friends sometimes," to which Sarah responds by quoting Maggie: "There is always something to miss, no matter where you are" (*Sarah*, 43). The simple reply acknowledges her kinship with Maggie as well as her acceptance of the fundamental truth of the sentiment. That there are always things to miss is the result of life's inevitable changes, and this book, like most of MacLachlan's books, is about change and the way to embrace it.

Partly because of Maggie's advice and partly because of her own independent spirit, Sarah insists on learning how to ride a horse and to drive a wagon so that she can go to town by herself. This alarms Caleb, for he fears Sarah is planning a means of escape. But before the lessons can take place, a squall strikes, Mother Nature at her most vicious. They all take shelter in the barn with the animals, and Sarah comes with an armful of roses, bringing comfort and calm. She notes that Maine has squalls "just like this." As with the haystack "dune," we are shown the similarities of seascape and landscape. The fierce sky over the prairie is the same looming presence in the midwest as it is over the eastern seacoast. Then hail falls and covers the ground, "white and gleaming for as far as [they] looked, like sun on glass. Like the sea" (*Sarah*, 50). Sarah, Caleb, and Anna must dwell on the similarities, not the differences. The similarities will draw them together and give them the bond they all desire.

Perhaps the one moment of real tension comes near the close of the story when Sarah drives the wagon to town by herself. Caleb is certain that Sarah wants to leave them, and he proposes to Anna that he get sick to induce Sarah to stay. Then, in desperation, he suggests tying her up. Anna flatly says no on both accounts, and Caleb at last breaks into tears. Anna shares his distress. They both fear they will suffer yet another loss in their lives. In Sarah's absence, Caleb searches for answers—he is too loud and pesky, the house is too small. But their fears are not realized, and Sarah returns from town with a small package for them containing three colored pencils—blue and gray and green. Caleb proclaims that "Sarah has brought the sea!" (*Sarah*, 57). Sarah, who is always forthright, tells them that she will always miss her old home, "but the truth of it is I would miss you more" (*Sarah*, 57). The book closes with an almost poetic passage that points to the future, a future that will hold a wedding; the coming seasons, autumn and winter; nests of curls and dried flowers; the animals, of course; and "Sarah's sea, blue and gray and green, hanging on the wall. And songs, old ones and new. And Seal with yellow eyes. And there will be Sarah, plain and tall" (*Sarah,* 58). The accumulated images are perfectly suited to the ending of a book that is so dominated by sensory imagery, a book that relies so heavily on intimations.

Much of the sensory imagery is found in MacLachlan's references to art, so pervasive in her work. Here it is in the singing, participated in and enjoyed by the entire family, and in Sarah's drawing. Through the music and the drawing, MacLachlan's characters share their vision of the world and of life. As is typical in MacLachlan's work, art is both an individual and a communal experience. The rhythm of its language undulates like the prairie grasses in the wind; the images stand forth stark and crystalline against the wide Western sky; and the design is simple, straightforward and sure like the Wittings' house on the plains. *Sarah, Plain and Tall* is an exquisite celebration of the family and the beauty of human relationships.

Sarah, Plain and Tall, the Screenplay

The Hallmark Hall of Fame presentation of "Sarah, Plain and Tall" (1990), starring Glenn Close in the title role, has probably brought the greatest fame to MacLachlan. It certainly widened her audience. When invited to write the screenplay, MacLachlan's task was to stretch a novella of under 60 pages into a full-blown, made-for-television event of nearly two hours. This is the reverse of the typical screen adaptation, which generally requires massive cutting from the original. The characters had to be fleshed out and the conflict required more dramatic flare, with an additional appeal to adults, the principal audience for the production. In this project, MacLachlan was assisted by Carol Sobieski, an experienced screenwriter who was assigned by the studio. The work, however, is largely MacLachlan's, as anyone familiar with her style can readily see.

Among the most important changes from book to screenplay is the narrative point of view. Anna no longer tells the story. That task is given over to an omniscient narrator, a format more suitable to handling the love interest between Sarah and Jacob.

Although Caleb remains essentially the same character as in the book, Anna's character is changed significantly. The screenplay Anna, who still grieves for her dead mother, sees Sarah as a threat, as someone who Anna believes is attempting to replace her mother. "She won't be my mother. She can be Caleb's. Not mine." The reason for Anna's prolonged grief can be found, in part, in her father's refusal to come to terms with his wife's death (still another element added to the screenplay). He has put away all her mementos and refuses to allow Anna those memories. At one point, Anna breaks down in Sarah's arms and confesses her fear that at times she can no longer remember what her mother looked like. The Anna of the screenplay also has nightmares—and has had them, we learn, since her mother's death. This development of Anna's character, although different from that in the book, is quite believable and does build on Anna's cautiousness and tentative nature that we see in the book.

Dovetailing this development of Anna's character is the extension of Sarah's character. One of the questions MacLachlan tried to answer was what would induce Sarah to leave her happy home in Maine for a life with strangers in a new and very different place. She decided to give Sarah an experience similar to that of Anna and Caleb's—that is, having lost, at an early age, her own mother. Picking up on this idea, Glenn Close wrote to MacLachlan: "No matter how wonderful her aunts are she has always longed for the intimacy of the mother she lost. She, too, has felt abandoned and betrayed. Somewhere inside her is a child like Anna who has yet to mourn."[2] Despite this inner, unspoken pain (or perhaps because of it), Sarah is a strong, self-willed individual, ready to share her life and love.

MacLachlan also recognized that somehow the suspense of whether or not Sarah would stay had to be deepened. Thus, MacLachlan introduced conflict between Sarah and Jacob in the form of Jacob's unassuaged grief and the haunting memories of his dead wife, Catherine, who had been his childhood sweetheart. It is Jacob's inability to accept her death that prevents him from reaching out to Sarah. His unresolved grief is symbolized by his refusal to plant flowers on Catherine's grave, for that would be acknowledging the finality of her death. (We are reminded of Sarah's planting flowers near the farmhouse—in both the book and the screenplay—suggesting her intention to make her stay permanent, to see the flowers grow and return another year.) Jacob has also insisted that all visible signs of Catherine's presence in the house be put away—the pictures she painted, her candlesticks, her quilt—all things that would preserve her memory for Anna and Caleb.

Sarah soon recognizes the problem, and in one dramatic moment she raises her voice to Jacob: "Catherine's not coming back." Jacob, equally stubborn, refuses to allow her to retrieve Catherine's things from the trunk where they have been hidden: "What is right in my house is what I say is right." Of course, Sarah ignores his dictum and removes the items from the trunk anyway. After all, Sarah had warned Jacob in her letter, "I am not mild-mannered." She also helps Anna and Caleb plant flowers on their mother's grave. It is Sarah's stubbornness that forces Jacob to face his sorrow and to deal with it.

In the screenplay, the neighbor Maggie is no longer a mail-order bride—a change intended to emphasize the uniqueness of Sarah's role in the story. A significant difference in the screenplay is that Maggie is pregnant. It is a difficult birth, and it falls to Jacob to take control of the situation, an experience that painfully recalls for him the tragedy of Catherine's death. This inclusion adds drama to the screenplay that is lacking in the book—although we should not interpret this as a weakness in the book. After his successful delivery of Maggie's baby, Jacob comes to better understand his own struggling feelings about birth and death. MacLachlan notes that this scene "is symbolic of his taking control of his life . . . and of his memories."[3]

Eventually, as a result of the accumulated efforts of Sarah and the children, Jacob is able to let go of Catherine's memory and give his heart to Sarah. She goes off to town on her own as in the book, but Anna discovers that the one-way train ticket to Maine that Sarah had purchased immediately upon her arrival is missing. Jacob jumps on a horse and races to town to find her, where he happily discovers that she has only cashed in her ticket. They melt into a predictably passionate embrace. The final image of the film is a slow-motion sequence of Sarah and Jacob's wedding.

The work exhibits the usual high quality of the Hallmark programs and preserves the quiet sensitivity of MacLachlan's story. Glenn Close is particularly well suited to the role of Sarah. Lexi Randall's Anna is quite good and captures some of the fine nuances of the character, but Christopher Bell's Caleb is perhaps too precious, his appearance almost doll-like and his dialogue at times cloyed in its delivery. Christopher Walken's Jacob certainly looks the part, although his character verges on the morose in his silently borne grief. In fact, he is so laconic and reserved in manner that we may wonder what possessed him to place the advertisement for a new wife in the first place—particularly if he still carried so fervently the torch for Catherine. The motivation for Jacob's invitation to Sarah seems to be undercut by his reluctance to have anyone replace his late wife. Despite the added material, the film contains many dead spots, a few too many silent stares and pregnant pauses. With its sparse prose, the book eschews sentimentalism; but with the addition of orchestral music and Technicolor, sentimentality can hardly be avoided in the film. Nevertheless, the production does capture much of the original spirit of the book, for both celebrate life's simple virtues and imbue the characters with grace and dignity.

Skylark, the Screenplay and the Book

Skylark is unique among MacLachlan's works in that it was first a screenplay, written for the 1992 Hallmark Hall of Fame production as a sequel to the screenplay of Sarah, Plain and Tall. It was Glenn Close and the cast of "Sarah" who persuaded MacLachlan to do the sequel; they wished to take advantage of the wave of popularity the first production enjoyed. The book did not appear until 1994, and as is to be expected, it follows the screenplay quite faithfully, the few emendations accommodating a younger audience. MacLachlan found the experience of transforming a screenplay into a book less satisfying than the other way around, undoubtedly because the process required a dilution of the original in order to make it suitable for a much younger audience. She found it difficult to summon up the inspiration she needed a second time around—a typical problem with "movie books." She decided that she would never again undertake such a task, preferring to write the book first and the screenplay second.

The television production includes the same cast as "Sarah" along with the necessary additions (we meet Sarah's aunts and brother, for example). It is the story of Sarah and Jacob's struggle to survive a disastrous drought shortly after their wedding. With the well having gone dry and a fire having destroyed the barn and threatened their home, Jacob insists that Sarah and the children go to Maine to stay with Sarah's aunts until the crisis is past. When the rains do come, Jacob finally travels to Maine to bring them home. The separation has convinced Sarah of her deep love for Jacob and her determination to stay on the prairie where she wants their baby to be born.

In writing the book for children, MacLachlan eliminated much of the discussion of Sarah's pregnancy (we do not learn about it until the end of the story). Because Anna narrates the story, the romantic exchanges between Sarah and Jacob are necessarily omitted. The story opens with a brief reminiscence of Sarah and Jacob's wedding under a cloudless sky—a symbol at once of the promise of happiness and of the peculiar cruelty of the midwestern landscape. Then a drought settles upon the land and the cloudless sky comes to signify the threat of starvation and the separation of the family. As one by one, their wells dry up, settlers pack their belongings and head back east. But the determined tenacity of Jacob will not permit him to succumb to defeat: "We'd never leave. . . . We were born here. Our names are written in this land" (*Skylark,* 6). Caleb, as always, clever beyond his years, confides to Anna that "Sarah wasn't born here." In a desperate attempt to fix fate, Caleb takes a stick and writes "SARA" in the dirt. Anna, always the realist, simply notes that he has misspelled her name. It is, after all, Sarah who must write her own name in the land.

Another thread running through the story is that of pregnancy and birth. Early in the story we learn that Seal, the cat, is pregnant, and a cow has a calf that the family names Moonbeam. In the screenplay, a scene depicts Sarah and Jacob aiding the calf's difficult breech birth, an experience that endears the calf to the family. This episode is left out of the book, since Anna, the narrator, does not witness the harrowing event and logically could not relate the details. Sarah proclaims, "I am surrounded by motherhood" (*Skylark*, 15). These births are symbols of hope as well as of the cycle of life and, of course, foreshadow Sarah's own pregnancy.

Sarah, who had previously shared Jacob's determination, begins to waiver in her commitment to the land. Her aunts in Maine send letters bearing news of storms and rainfall greening the landscape—in sharp contrast to the oppressive brown of the dry prairie grasses. Sarah confides her frustration to Maggie: "Jacob once said his name was written in this land, but mine isn't. It isn't" (*Skylark*, 40). Maggie then compares Sarah to the prairie lark: "It sings its song above the land to let all the birds know it's there before it plunges down to earth to make its home. But you have not come to earth, Sarah. . . . You don't have to love this land. . . . But if you don't love it, you won't survive. Jacob's right. You have to write your name in the land to live here" (*Skylark*, 40). Sarah does not respond but only takes a handful of the dry prairie grass and lets it crumble symbolically through her fingers.

A birthday celebration for Sarah temporarily relieves the looming sense of desperation. The aunts have sent a phonograph and the family enjoys music and dancing. Anna gives Sarah a book she has written about their family that begins "When my mother, Sarah, came, she came by train" (*Skylark*, 49). The book signifies Anna's complete acceptance of Sarah as her mother. But it represents something more, for now we see Anna as an artist. As always with MacLachlan, art is a means of personal expression; just as Sarah best conveys her feelings through her singing, dancing, and drawing, Anna has now found a way of articulating and sharing her innermost thoughts through the written word. In her book Anna has written, "My mother, Sarah, doesn't love the prairie. She tries, but she can't help remembering what she knew first" (*Skylark*, 49). MacLachlan recalls talking to a group of elementary school children about *Sarah, Plain and Tall* and showing them, as part of her presentation, a bag of prairie dirt she had brought from her childhood home. One child observed, "You should keep the bag on your window because that's what you knew first."[4] She was so struck by the comment that the expression—"what you know first"—would resurface in *Skylark* and eventually become transformed into the title of a picture book. The ultimate message is that although we will not forget what we knew first, it is sometimes necessary to move beyond that to find fulfillment and happiness. This is the lesson Sarah must learn. Brief passages from Anna's journal are inserted between the chapters, and they serve to establish the mood of the succeeding chapter. Typically they convey simple yet powerful images drawn from the family's everyday experiences: the sweet, sharp smell of the earth; the wildflowers hanging from the ceiling to dry; the hair cuttings tossed into the fields for the birds to use for nests; joyful walks through the rows of corn; and "the sky so big it takes your breath away, the land like a giant quilt tossed out" (*Skylark*, 87). These journal passages contain some of the most poetic language of the book, and they establish mood and give the story immediacy. They are not found in the screenplay.

The joy of the birthday celebration is all too brief, for Matthew and Maggie's well dries up, and they are forced to leave. Hard upon that disappointment comes the fire that destroys the Witting barn. It is decided that Sarah will take the children and go to Maine for the duration of the drought. The decision is very unsettling to the children, who have seen Sarah grow more and more miserable with the desperate circumstances, and they fear that she will not want to return to the prairie once she is safely back in Maine.

The train takes them to Maine (in the film the station sign reads Camden, but the book provides no geographical hints except to say that it is in Maine by the sea). Sarah announces when she steps off the train that she is "back to what I knew first" (*Skylark*, 58). In Maine we meet the aunts, at last. MacLachlan is particularly good at portraying old people, and she seems clearly in her element describing the delightfully eccentric maiden women: Aunt Mattie, barefoot and in silk; Aunt Harriet, tall with wire glasses; and Aunt Lou, in overalls and high boots, who likes to go skinny-dipping. All three are robust, gregarious, and in love with life, in the spirit of such MacLachlan characters as Aunt Elda, Cassie Binegar's Gran, and the Unclaimed Treasures. (In fact, they are referred to as "unclaimed treasures" in *Sarah, Plain and Tall* and simply as the "treasures" in the screenplay of *Skylark*.) The aunts are also artists: Harriet plays a squeaky flute, Lou plays the piano, and Mattie dances.

Whereas in *Sarah, Plain and Tall* we see the similarities in the landscapes of the seacoast and the prairie, in *Skylark* we see the differences. The heavily forested New England landscape is closed in, although the ocean offers the same sense of space as does the Western grassland. Maine is also closer to civilization. It is older and more settled—"full of voices and people laughing and talking," as Anna writes (*Skylark*, 62). It is full of carefully tended gardens, and flowers the children had never seen before. There Anna and Caleb have their first ride in a motor car. It is presented as a land of temptations—although it is not evil except that it threatens to entice Sarah and the children away from their comparatively impoverished homeland.

But the temptation is not so great as it first seems to Anna. Sarah's brother William plays a minor role, but it is in a conversation with him that Sarah recalls a song their father used to sing, a song about a skylark. William remarks, "I only remember the first line: 'Like a skylark Sarah sings!' Papa said you'd never come to earth" (*Skylark*, 72). The fact that Sarah's family recognized in her the same restless quality that her friend Maggie had noted merely confirms that her reluctance to put down roots has been in her nature. Or, to use the language of the story, Sarah's name had never been written in the land of the Maine coast. Sarah's spirit is bold and searching; it is this spirit that drove her to leave her Maine home in the first place and embark on a new adventure in the barely tamed West. But there comes a time when even the lark must come to earth.

And so it is that, for both the children and for Sarah, the Maine household is full of life, beauty, and wisdom, but it is not home. The exchange of letters between Sarah and the children in Maine and Jacob back on the farm is an obvious inversion of the circumstances at the beginning of *Sarah, Plain and Tall*. The letters are all simple and direct; what is left unsaid is nearly as important as what is said. The power of words—spoken and written—is another thread running through the narrative of *Skylark*. Of Jacob's first letters to her before they were married, Sarah says that "I loved what was between the lines most." When Caleb asks what was between the lines, Sarah replies, "His life . . . That was what was between the lines" (*Skylark,* 11). Sarah also says that "Sometimes, what people choose to write down on paper is more important than what they say," a comment intended for Anna who is hard at work writing in her journal. And now that they are in Maine, far away from Jacob, they must rely on the written words again. The letters they write betray their longing to be reunited, but almost always this is revealed in what is left unsaid, what is between the lines.

As time passes, the children fear that Sarah will not want to return to the prairie. They become especially anxious when Sarah speaks of enrolling them in school in Maine. This is one of the few elements that appears in the book but not in the screenplay, demonstrating the screenplay's focus on the adults, the book's focus on the children. But in August Jacob shows up unannounced and with characteristic directness says to Sarah, "It rained" (*Skylark,* 81). In the screenplay, a romantic scene follows between Sarah and Jacob in which she tells him she is pregnant and that she came to Maine "to stay long enough to say goodbye." It is clear that Sarah and Jacob's child will be a child of the prairie, further tying Sarah to the land. Indeed, upon her arrival back at the farm, Sarah immediately picks up a stick and scrawls her name in the prairie dirt.

The final passage in the book is from Anna's journal and describes the green beauty of Maine set alongside the prairie with its "sky so big it takes your breath away, the land like a giant quilt tossed out" (*Skylark,* 87). The conclusion is reminiscent of the lyrical ending to *Sarah, Plain and Tall*:

> It will rain again. There is some water in the pond. Not enough for swimming, but there will be. There will be flowers in the

spring, and the river will run again. And in the spring there will be the new baby, Papa and Sarah's baby.

Caleb, like Papa, is not always good with words. But I think Caleb says it best.

Our baby. (*Skylark*, 87)

The screenplay does not include these tender passages from the journal, and it is the poorer for that. The screenplay suffers in much the same way that the screenplay for *Sarah* suffers—both are overly sentimental, too slow paced, and too predictable. In the screenplays, fans of MacLachlan will miss the poetic beauty of her language and the clarity of her imagery that are so central to her books, books that some may feel need no illustrating, certainly no embellishment.

Assessment

Both *Sarah, Plain and Tall* and *Skylark* are related to two important literary traditions—the historical novel and the family story. But to call these novels historical novels is granting a liberality to the term that some critics would not admit. Jill Paton Walsh once defined the historical novel as one that is "wholly or partly about the public events and social conditions which are the material of history."[5] She distinguishes this from the sort of book that is simply set in some past time, but whose story and theme are essentially nonhistorical (she uses the unfortunate term "costume drama"). *Sarah, Plain and Tall* and *Skylark* are surely of this latter type. MacLachlan is not especially interested in "public events and social conditions," and her historical setting is largely a backdrop, chosen primarily because the germinal story of the mail-order bride was taken from her family's past. Contrary to most works of historical fiction, the specific time and place are not important to either of these books (only the film *Sarah* provides us with an exact date—1910). The place is equally vague (once again the films inform us the setting is Kansas and Camden, Maine, but that information is not revealed in the books nor is it particularly crucial). More important for younger readers, who have only a vague sense of history and geography, is this capturing of a sense of place and of an earlier time. The isolated life on a pioneer farm, the simple machinery, and the reliance on horses and homegrown gardens are all concepts that are fairly easy for readers in the intermediate grades to grasp.

The appeal of pioneering days for younger readers is a phenomenon as true today as it was when Laura Ingalls Wilder's *Little House* books were first published in the 1930s. (In the 1980s, a popular series of rather expensive dolls based on nineteenth-century American girls was introduced, complete with fashionable garments and elaborate accessories, attesting to the perennial fascination with the American past.) It seems unlikely that children would be drawn to these portrayals of the past out of nostalgia, and so for children at least, their appeal must lie elsewhere. Much of the attraction of these stories may lie in their celebration of individualism; in the opportunities they offer their heroes and heroines to prove themselves against seemingly tremendous odds; and perhaps from the child's point of view, in the independence their young characters enjoy, unshackled by the trappings of society. In few modern settings, for example, could parents go off to town and safely leave their young children alone on the farm (that a similar event occurs in *Arthur, for the Very First Time* only suggests that *Arthur* is set in a somewhat earlier time in this century). And in no modern setting would a 10-year-old girl be expected to bake the family bread and carry out the myriad of chores necessary to keep a pioneer homestead operating (admittedly activities more fun to read about and to imagine than to engage in). But at the same time, it is not the strength of the individual alone that enables survival—it the strength of the family. MacLachlan is an heir of Laura Ingalls Wilder in her unbounded faith in the family. For both writers, the family, braced by love, nurtures civilization. And as with all good novels, historical or otherwise, the fundamental truths of the stories transcend the time period in which they are set. The stories celebrate familial bonds, joys and sorrows, loves and labors, all with the home at the center of life and living. Like the Ingalls family, the Wittings are the family we all long for—with kind, strong, and sensitive parents and understanding and caring siblings. MacLachlan's romantic view of the family belongs to an old American literary tradition and fosters a dream that, however dim, we have not yet lost.

MacLachlan does not lament the loss of a pristine society nor does she unduly praise the simple life on the Western prairie or on the Maine coast. Landscapes are important, of course; they claim our affections in powerful ways, and they, with equal strength, determine the course of our lives. In *Sarah, Plain and Tall* we see the similarities between the seacoast and the prairie, and in *Skylark* we see the differences, and we come to understand why the Wittings choose one over the other. But their choice is not a matter of birthright or even of preference for one landscape over another. Rather, human relationships matter the most, as is reflected in Sarah's confession to the children, "I will always miss my old home, but the truth of it is I would miss you more" (*Sarah*, 57). In *Skylark*, Sarah returns to Maine to test the strength of her loyalties and affections, and she happily learns that they now lie with her new family and new home on the prairie. As if to cement that loyalty, her new baby will be a child of the prairie. Many similarities exist between MacLachlan and Wilder, including their simple and direct style, the clarity of their imagery, and their steady focus on the family unit. But unlike Pa Ingalls, who is always on the move, just one step ahead of encroaching civilization, the Wittings determine to place their roots in the land that can be so harsh a mistress, the land that they call home. The message emerging so assuredly from these books is that the bonds of family, home, and the landscape are powerful indeed, for from them we draw strength of character and learn the wisdom of love. MacLachlan's journey to the past gives us a glimpse of the future, for as she says: "As we touch and affect the lives of those we love— friends, family, and children if we have them—we become, in some ways, the roots of the future. I have always liked this notion of an on-going circle, though I've never felt it touch me so closely as in the writing of *Sarah, Plain and Tall*."[6]

Chapter Five

The Later Novels:
The Facts and Fictions of
Minna Pratt, Journey, and *Baby*

Facts and fictions are different kinds of truth.
—*The Facts and Fictions of Minna Pratt*

Following *Sarah, Plain and Tall*, MacLachlan once again turned to writing contemporary fiction, and she began to experiment with narrative structures and voices. The three contemporary novels (the term *contemporary* is used loosely since MacLachlan deliberately obscures the time period in her books) that succeed *Sarah, Plain and Tall* exhibit some distinctly new directions from the three that precede *Sarah*. The first distinction is a newfound preference for the first-person narrator. Of the five novels beginning with *Sarah*, only *The Facts and Fictions of Minna Pratt* is written in the third person—and that book, as we shall see, uses a variety of narrative techniques. (It is also interesting to note that the three picture books she has written since *Minna Pratt* are also first-person narratives.) MacLachlan became much more comfortable with the narrative voice of the youthful protagonist and discovered that the first-person narrative was especially suited to the confessional nature of her fiction. *Journey* and *Baby* are the most obviously confessional stories; the protagonists freely bare their souls for us, showing us their failings and allowing us to share in their troubled ascent to a new level of maturity. The first-person narrative provides more immediacy and allows the reader an easier identification with the protagonist.

The second important distinction is that the novels following *Sarah* reveal MacLachlan's desire to explore more traumatic themes—the breakup of a family, the abandonment of children, death, and bereavement. And particularly in *Journey* and *Baby,* she moves away from the tidy endings that typify her early works. In the earlier novels, the emphasis was, to paraphrase St. Francis, on changing the things we can; whereas in the later novels, it is on accepting the things we cannot change. For the purposes of convenience, the following discussion will focus only on the three contemporary novels written since *Sarah.* We should keep in mind that *Skylark* appeared in book form after *Journey* and that MacLachlan published several picture books following *The Facts and Fictions of Minna Pratt,* all of which have previously been discussed.

The Facts and Fictions of Minna Pratt

MacLachlan's love of music achieves its fullest expression in *The Facts and Fictions of Minna Pratt* (1988). Indeed, the novel itself is like a musical score, the narrative passages playing variations as they alternate between the past and present tense; the clashing dissonance created by the contrast between the cold, immaculate upper-class home of the Ellerbys and the warm, messy comfort of the unpretentious Pratts; and the final harmony achieved in the concert hall at the music competition. But it is largely a quiet piece of music, for this is the most uneventful of MacLachlan's novels—even *Sarah, Plain and Tall* has its storm and its moments of anxious waiting. In *Minna Pratt* we observe the minutiae of daily living. We anticipate the time when (not if) Minna, a cellist, will get her vibrato. We wonder how Minna will arrive at the realization that her parents are, in fact, charming in their eccentricity and all the better for that. We are anxious to see what will come of Minna's growing relationship with the sensitive Lucas.

The plot is episodic, as MacLachlan's plots tend to be, with the episodes tied together by Minna's search for her vibrato and the preparation of her string quartet for the big music competition. The action of the novel is simple: Minna meets Lucas Ellerby, a violist and the newest member of her chamber group; they develop a close friendship; she goes to his house for dinner, he goes to hers, they prepare for the music competition while Minna seeks ways of achieving her vibrato; and they win the competition despite Minna's lack of a vibrato. MacLachlan introduces her usual assortment of delightfully eccentric characters: Willie, a hip street musician full of wise advice; Lewis, a gregarious bus driver who shares a personal interest in his passengers; Twig, the Ellerbys' unconventional housekeeper, who is an aspiring artist from a Vermont sheep farm working her way through school and who eventually gets hooked up with Willie; Minna's younger brother McGrew, wise beyond his years; and McGrew's friend, the baseball-playing Emily Parmalee, wildly uninhibited in both her manner and dress. In addition to Lucas and Minna, the chamber group includes Imelda, the first violinist who is an encyclopedia of useless information; Orson, the second violinist who is in love with words; and Porch, the dedicated string teacher who finally lights on the idea of having the players face the wall during their practice so they can focus on their own music alone.

Completing the cast of characters are Minna's parents, her father a psychologist and her mother a writer (exactly as in the MacLachlan household), who have an ideal marriage. Minna, however, is embarrassed by her mother's deplorable housekeeping (the clean laundry never makes it out of the baskets and into the drawers, and Minna's feet stick to the kitchen floor, "making sucking sounds as she walked" (19). She is equally embarrassed by her father, who loves bad jokes, classical music (which he conducts to recordings in his study), and positively everything about his wife. He is particularly good natured when it comes to her housekeeping, joking that "they were all in danger of death due to lint buildup" (18). Minna is embarrassed by her parents because they are different. She longs to have parents like Lucas's. The Ellerbys, counterparts of Margaret's mother in *Cassie Binegar*, are rich, stuffy, and appear on the surface the models of perfection. They live in an immaculate house where even "the dinner conversation can be divided into headings on three-by-five cards, all lined" (95). But like Margaret's mother, they are distant parents, often lacking in real understanding of their son's needs.

Facts and Fictions is an unusual book for MacLachlan on several counts, the most obvious of which is its setting. The story takes place in the city during the spring when school is still in session. MacLachlan abandoned her usual rural summer location largely out of necessity—the novel had to be set near a string studio and during the school year, since the events were to lead up to a recital. Still, the city setting is remarkably placid—even exhaust fumes from a noisy bus are described as "warm puffs" (27). Minna's parents are professionals, and Lucas's are just plain rich. Both families lives in houses, not apartments. It is, in other words, a rather pastoral urban environment. Minna's house is a book lover's paradise. There are books everywhere within arm's reach. It is comfortable, warm, and delightfully disheveled. One must clear away the books and papers to find a place to eat at the dining table. It is a stimulating household.

The setting during the school year does give MacLachlan an opportunity to portray a schoolteacher. Minna's teacher is Miss Barbizon (the name is reminiscent of Barbie dolls or perhaps of the once famous modeling school and seems to suggest someone of vapid intellect). She is rigid and unimaginative, and she has the students write stories employing assigned vocabulary words, like *cachinnate, nettlesome,* and *ozone.* She insists that "every story must have a beginning, a middle, and an end" (26). This is the same advice an elementary-school teacher of MacLachlan's once gave to her. It is one of the few memories of MacLachlan's school days to find its way into her books. This unflattering portrait of a schoolteacher will be balanced with the wise and sensitive Ms. Minifred, the teacher-librarian in MacLachlan's later novel, *Baby.*

The vocabulary instruction that Miss Barbizon drills into the children does, however, complement one of the major themes of the book—the power (and occasionally the failure) of language. Language is a further interest for second violinist Orson, who is always bringing new words to rehearsals, such as *rebarbative* and *sapient,* challenging the group to use them. His conviction is that words are power. Minna's mother, naturally in love with words and language, pins provoking messages on her bulletin board along with letters from her young readers. (The letters are all taken from actual correspondence that MacLachlan received from her own readers and secured permission for before using. They are delightfully frank and not always flattering; one girl wrote, "My class has to write to a book writer. I wanted to write to Beatrix Potter or Mark Twain but they are dead, so I'm writing to you [20].) Among the messages is one that Minna finds particularly perplexing: "Facts and fictions are different kinds of truths." It sounds like double-talk to her, and she is annoyed that her mother would even post it. Minna's search for the meaning of this cryptic message will become an obsession.

Imelda plays another variation on this theme of fact and fiction, for she is a veritable storehouse of useless facts that she is wont to distribute freely, whether anyone is listening or not. Consequently, Imelda helps Minna discover the relationship between fact and fiction, truth and lie. It is interesting that the first "fact" that Imelda relates is itself a fiction that was once popularly believed: "Have you heard the fact . . . that the great wall of China is actually visible from the moon?" (11). Whether or not MacLachlan knew the "truth" of this "fact" at the time of the writing is immaterial. The message remains: Language is often inadequate in conveying the truly important things. And language for its own sake, as in Orson's $64 words, can be as useless as Imelda's facts. But at the book's outset, Minna does not yet realize all this. Her response to Imelda's fact is *"I wish I'd thought of that fine fact. Then Lucas would have smiled at me"* (12). Fortunately for Minna, Lucas is not nearly so shallow as that.

Facts and Fictions is in many respects a very esoteric novel. The musical references are undoubtedly beyond the ken of most 11- and 12-year-olds, and sadly, but surely, very few could identify with Minna's devotion to classical music. Much of the following passage, for example, would be lost on the average sixth grader:

She walked up the last flight of stairs, slowly, slowly thinking of yesterday's lesson. It was Bartók, bowing hand for Bartók staccato; swift, short bow, Porch's hand on her elbow, forcing her wrist to do the work. When she got it right, he would smile his Bartók smile: there quickly, then gone. It would be early Haydn today. High third finger, she reminded herself, digging her thumbnail into the finger, forcing it to remember. After Haydn it would be

the Mozart. *The Mozart. K. 157.* The number was etched on her
mind, and Minna stopped suddenly, her breath caught in her
throat. The Mozart with the terrible andante she couldn't play.
The andante her fingers didn't know, *wouldn't* know. And then the
wild presto that left her trembling. (8)

Its esoteric nature is, in part, the product of the author's own deep
commitment to her subject. MacLachlan is an avid musician, a
cellist, in fact. She used to accompany her children to music
lessons, taking along her own cello so she could play along with
the youth orchestra during their rehearsals. She recalls that her
primary function at those rehearsals was to sit in the back with the
budding cellists and try to keep them in tempo. Only a great lover
of music could write this story, and it is one of the few books available for young readers that describes the excitement, indeed the
ecstasy, of playing a great piece of music:

> It is a bit like dying, Minna thinks, or so she's heard. All the
> things she must remember, all the things she has learned pass by
> in her mind's eye: the fortes, the pianissimos, the difficult bowing
> parts she has checked in pencil on her music, the fingering. She
> nearly forgets the first repeat, somehow. Lucas, next to her, looks
> at her and smiles because he knows it. The allegro ends, and some-
> one in the balcony applauds and is quickly hushed by a sister, a
> brother, a wife. Imelda smiles. Orson tunes. Minna takes a breath.
> The andante. Minna waits through her measures of rests, looking
> out to find Porch. But she can't see him in the dark. Minna smiles
> at this; places her bow on the strings. Begins. Strangely, Minna
> thinks about it later, the andante seems to come from her fingers
> for the very first time, not from her head. Her fingers stretch with-
> out her telling them to stretch. They have learned the music. They
> know Mozart. (131)

This, of course, has been Minna's goal; knowing the music is more
important than having a vibrato.

But although the subject is music, the theme of *Facts and Fictions* is very similar to that of *Unclaimed Treasures* and *Cassie Binegar.* It is a coming-of-age novel, a fact announced in the book's

opening pages: "Minna Pratt, age eleven, is sitting patiently next to her cello waiting to be a woman" (3). Her achieving a vibrato becomes a metaphor for maturity—it is something she must experience and not discover—it must emerge from within her being and not be imposed from without. Willie, a street musician from whom Minna seeks advice about her vibrato, tells her: "Sometimes it's unexpected. Almost natural and hardly noticed, like your eyebrows growing. And sometimes it comes as a great surprise after a lot of hard work . . . Like becoming an adult" (76). One critic points out that finding the vibrato is frequently couched in almost sexual terms. Lucas tells Minna, "I got it at music camp" (13). *Facts and Fictions* includes more overt sexual implications and innuendos than MacLachlan's previous works, and musical terms most often provide the language of sexuality. We are told that Minna typically "eases into love as she eases into a Bach cello suite, slowly and carefully, frowning all the way" (11). And the wonderful description of the string quartet performance at the book's conclusion is almost orgasmic.

Unlike Cassie and Willa, Minna does not develop a crush on an older man—although she confesses to having done so in the past. In fact, her relationship with Lucas, whom we clearly perceive as a boyfriend and a particularly well-suited one at that, is curiously unromantic—they behave as bosom friends, much like McGrew and Emily Parmalee, rather than as prospective lovers. But the book is not so much about Minna's sexual awareness as it is about her psychological maturity, her coming to terms with the conflict with her mother and the discovery of her own self-confidence and individuality. MacLachlan acknowledges that this book grew out of a period when she and her 14-year old daughter were engaged in the typical conflicts that beset teenagers and their parents. The conflicts passed, as they normally do, but MacLachlan's response to life's challenges has always been to write about them. *Facts and Fictions* is a more contemplative book than MacLachlan's previous works, and the narrative technique is designed to convey the turbulent emotions Minna experiences. The passages shift in tense between past and present, with the narrative in the beginning of the book tending more heavily toward the past tense and the concluding chapters surrendering totally to the present tense. At times the choice of past or present seems purely arbitrary, but the shifting serves to reflect the unsettled state of Minna's mind, her ambivalence toward her parents, particularly her mother, and her romantic feelings about Lucas. The past tense is the language of the detached observer, the present tense that of the involved insider. Roberta Trites[1] has pointed out that MacLachlan's female protagonists between the ages of 10 and 12 have all been silenced by external forces (usually related, Trites says, to repressive patriarchal traditions), and all must achieve a self-awareness that will help them give voice to their feelings and to emerge from their cultural silencing. The gradual transformation from the detached past-tense narrative to the participatory present-tense narrative rhetorically suggests Minna's emergence from her cultural silence, when she was only an observer of the events surrounding her, and her becoming a full-fledged participant in the affairs of her own life. In fact, toward the beginning of the novel, MacLachlan periodically inserts italicized passages representing Minna's interior monologues in which she fantasizes about a TV announcer commenting on her life. They are comical interludes, such as this one, comparing her forthcoming concert to her brother's baseball game: "ANNOUNCER: *Welcome, baseball fans, on a beautiful sunny afternoon where the Sox are here to play Mozart. Playing first fiddle is number 7 . . . the shortstop will play second . . . the left fielder will hum*" (74). By using these different narrative voices, MacLachlan emphasizes the exploratory nature of Minna's quest for self-understanding and a means of self-expression.

It should be noted, however, that Minna is silenced not by a male authority figure (as Cassie and Willa had been) but by her own mother, a writer who seems never to answer her questions directly, choosing instead to respond in riddles. Minna is annoyed by having her questions always answered with other questions and by the seemingly pointless questions her mother often raises, questions that appear to be completely off the topic of conversation. Like Cassie, Minna wishes her mother were more like other people's mothers, particularly like Emily Parmalee's mother whose floor is so clean you could eat off it. Or perhaps even like

Mrs. Ellerby who is always so together and organized. Minna comes to appreciate her mother when Twig's artistic pursuits come to light. The Ellerbys had no idea of Twig's talents, but Minna realizes: "My mother would have known. . . . She asks questions." To which Lucas replies, sadly, "Mine doesn't" (88). Lucas is silenced in a more real way than is Minna. His parents have no idea what he is about. They give him a room with plenty of space at the top of the house and never intrude (or show an interest). He harbors hundreds of frogs up there and they never know it (that is, until the frogs escape). Both Minna and Lucas keep their feelings bottled up inside them, in marked contrast to McGrew and Emily Parmalee, who are bold and forthright. Emily is proud of her pierced ears and displays ostentatious earrings even at her baseball games. At one game she wears earrings of pink feathers: "Emily's got her feathers," McGrew announces (56). We are reminded of Cassie Binegar's extroverted cousin Coralinda, who loved to dress in feathers; although unlike Coralinda, who hides personal anguish behind her feathers, Emily exudes a self-confidence in her bold attire.

The book is filled with comic scenes and comic characters—most of the characters seem to be caricatures, each character eccentric in his or her own way. We find comedy in the baskets of laundry overrunning the Pratt home (the Pratts find it necessary to purchase only plain white athletic socks since it becomes impossible to match up the stripes from the piles of clothes), in Twig's bizarre driving habits (her recklessness reminds us of Old Pepper's hair-raising trip to the hospital in *Unclaimed Treasures*), in the hundreds of frogs escaping from Lucas's room, in the comical letters from Mrs. Pratt's readers, and in the laughable pretensions of the Ellerbys. All these incidents border on the absurd or even on slapstick. The humor provides a counterbalance to the seriousness of the theme as well as to the rather intellectual passages about classical music, and the characters give tremendous warmth to the story.

But the comic scenes are ultimately displaced by the more serious aspects. Frequently throughout the novel, a spate of questions fills Minna's mind—and, like Cassie Binegar, she is unable to voice them. When Minna catches herself wondering about the street musician Willie, where he lives, if he has brothers and sisters, and what he thinks about, she suddenly realizes: "I am thinking just like my mother. It *is* catching!" (52). (This may be one of the most unsettling realizations for a young girl.) Her mother, she has noticed, always responds to her fan mail faithfully, even going so far as to research her answers. Consequently Minna, in desperation, decides to write a letter to her mother, a letter signed with a fictitious name and no address. This technique is a variation on the method Jason recommends to Cassie Binegar, and it reflects the writer's conviction that articulation is a key part of understanding. (The letters between Mrs. Pratt and her fans and Minna's own letter constitute still another narrative format that MacLachlan employs in the novel.) That Minna should feel she must resort to this tactic to communicate with her mother suggests a great deal about the state of the mother/daughter relationship—although it says more about Minna than her mother. The letter reads like the cry of the typical early adolescent: "My mother doesn't really hear what I say. She doesn't listen. She asks the wrong questions. She answers with the wrong answers" (67). And Mrs. Pratt recognizes the author of the letter immediately.

Eventually Minna comes to understand the meaning of the confusing aphorism—"Facts and fictions are different kinds of truths"—and when she does, she discovers the secret to her relationship with her mother and achieves a new level of self-awareness, confidence, and personal satisfaction. McGrew is fond of reciting bizarre headlines, such as those that might appear in the *National Enquirer*: "Scientist Says Madness Passed by Virus" (116) or "Housewife Can't Stop Eating Caterpillars" (125). These serve as perplexing aphorisms themselves—part fact, part fiction—and are corollaries to Imelda's storehouse of trivia. The point is that there is a connection between fact and fiction. When a young reader asks Mrs. Pratt, "Are [your stories] *all* lies?" she responds, "Some of them are and some of them are not. But they are *all* true" (124). In the typical MacLachlan novel, a myriad of images, seemingly insignificant incidents and references, ultimately merge into a bountiful whole. Few of her books are as rich and varied as

The Facts and Fictions of Minna Pratt. The episodic structure is designed around a series of small epiphanies by which a fuller understanding of the self and of the relationship between the self and the world is made possible. And the epiphanies do not only come to Minna. Lucas does not tell his parents about the music competition because he is afraid they will not make a fuss (conversely, Minna does not tell hers because she is afraid they will). Both Minna and Lucas misjudge their parents. Minna's parents do not embarrass her and Lucas's parents decide to host a backstage reception for the musicians—"Win or lose." And Lucas ironically remarks to Minna, "That's a bit of a fuss, don't you think?" (122). It is this sort of understatement at which MacLachlan excels. She closes the book with Minna's call to Lucas at 12:30 at night to tell him she has finally achieved her vibrato. Lucas lifts the phone on the first ring, and, before she can answer, he says simply, "Congratulations." Lucas has become a true friend, one she can call at any hour of the day or night and one who knows what is important to her. As readers, we also know that the congratulations is not for the vibrato alone; Minna has achieved much more, a significant step on the road to maturity.

Journey

MacLachlan's older son, John, is a professional photographer, and it is appropriate that *Journey* (1991) is dedicated to him, for photography plays a central role in this brief novel of loss and acceptance. In *Journey*, MacLachlan returns to the shorter form of *Sarah, Plain and Tall* and *Skylark*, and like those works the novel is characterized by an economy of precise language and evocative imagery to reinforce the theme. As in *The Facts and Fictions of Minna Pratt,* the story is one of reflection rather than action.

The story is one of MacLachlan's simplest in terms of plot development. Over the course of a summer, 11-year-old Journey is attempting to understand why his mother abandoned his sister, Cat, and him, leaving them with their grandparents, a farm couple. Wracked by a general anger toward the world, Journey, with the help of his understanding grandparents, comes to terms with his mother's desertion and is able to accept himself for who he is. As with several of MacLachlan's young protagonists, Journey is angry with his mother (he never really knew his father well enough to hate him). However, Journey's is a much more serious and harrowing situation than that of Arthur, Cassie, or Minna, whose quarrels with their parents are seldom more than minor piques or misunderstandings.

Like *Sarah, Plain and Tall* and *Skylark, Journey* is told through a first-person narrative; although the narrator in *Journey* is the central, dynamic character and not merely an observer and commentator, as Anna largely functioned in the earlier works. Once again, as in *The Facts and Fictions of Minna Pratt,* MacLachlan experiments with tense shifts, invoking more immediacy to those scenes written in the present tense and more reflection to those written in the past tense. The plot is episodic, again typical of MacLachlan's works, and it is one of the most heavily symbolic of her novels. The protagonist's name, Journey, gives the work an almost medieval allegorical quality—Journey is the human spirit in search of self-understanding. His is a journey from childhood innocence to adolescent understanding. The surface simplicity of the book disguises a deeply sensitive narrative, rich in meaning.

The setting is rural in the not-too-distant past. Grandmother notes she first met her future husband in 1930. This would seem to set the story somewhere in the 1970s or very early 1980s at the latest. But we also learn that Grandfather's car has a running board, making it a veritable antique—even for a story set 20 years ago. This story exudes the nostalgia of an earlier era. A great garden supplies the table, the world moves slowly, and outside forces seldom intrude (MacLachlan's fictional homes are most commonly without television). It is a simpler time, reflecting the aura many adult readers may recall from their childhoods.

In the first chapter we are introduced to Journey, whose mother has just recently left him and his sister, Catherine (called "Cat"), with their somewhat eccentric grandparents. They join MacLachlan's gallery of extraordinary and lovable seniors, dealing with the world boldly on their own terms. Grandfather is busy taking pictures, a newly acquired hobby that will become a predominant symbol in the story. Journey is generally annoyed with his grand-father—it is the annoyance of despondency faced with unwelcome cheer. Like Cassie and Minna, Journey is full of questions unan-swered: "What would pictures tell me of my grandmother, so secretive; my grandfather, tall and blunt?" And of the picture of his father on Cat's dresser, "The picture never told me the things I wanted to know. Did he think about Cat and me? Where was he? Would I know him if I saw him?" (4–5). We will never know, and Journey will never know, the answers to many of these ques-tions—just as in real life we pose questions that are never answered. If Journey is annoyed with his grandfather and his pho-tographic efforts, he is downright angry with his grandmother when she appears wearing his mother's shirt. This gesture symbol-izes for Journey his grandmother's acknowledgment that his mother's absence is permanent. His grandfather captures Jour-ney's anger in a photograph, which, Journey confesses, "would startle me every time I saw it: not Grandma, her hair tied back with a piece of string, smiling slightly as if she knew the secrets of the world; not Cat, her head thrown back, laughing; but my face, staring into the camera with such fury that even in the midst of the light and the laughter the focus of the picture is me" (6). And so we are presented with one of the predominant themes, the truths and fictions captured through the art of photography.

A lesser writer might have ultimately answered Journey's questions about his father and returned his wayward mother home to be reunited with her children. But despite her quaint characters and happy endings, MacLachlan is never the sentimen-talist. Her interest in *Journey* is how a child adjusts to abandon-ment by a parent, how a child comes to terms with the accompa-nying guilt and the conflicting feelings of love and hate. Abandonment of children is a theme that recurs almost obses-sively in MacLachlan's work—in *Mama One, Mama Two*, Maudie experiences a kind of abandonment when her mother suffers a mental breakdown; in *Arthur, for the Very First Time*, Moira has been abandoned by her parents; in *Cassie Binegar*, Cassie feels abandoned by her grandfather who died so suddenly; in *Unclaimed Treasures*, Horace's mother temporarily abandons her

family; in *Sarah, Plain and Tall*, Anna and Caleb both feel a sense
of abandonment by their mother (a sentiment more fully explored in the screenplay); and in *Baby*, written after *Journey*, an
infant is literally left in a basket on a doorstep. The theme of
abandonment seems to have no particularly personal repercus-
sions for MacLachlan (her own family life is almost exemplary).
Surely her experiences with the Children's Aid Family Service
Agency heightened her own awareness of the problem. But also,
MacLachlan sees abandonment or the fear of abandonment as a
haunting presence in the childhood experience. It is a psychological fear of perhaps primal origins, but it is certainly widespread in
Western civilization, where it is found in some of the earliest stories for children and is almost common in folktales: "Hansel and
Gretel" and "Rapunzel" are two of the most pointed, but the idea
emerges in one form or another in scores of tales.

   The hurt for Journey deepens when at last he and Cat receive
an envelope from their mother that contains only money and no
letter. There is no return address, and Journey, in a state of denial,
insists that "she forgot, that's all" (9). His wise and gentle grandmother shows Journey a family album and a picture of his mother
in her youth, a sad, silent girl who "always wished to be somewhere else" (12). The camera captured this disturbing quality—
"The camera knows," his grandmother tells him.

   Shortly after, Journey and Cat peruse the family photo album
with the neighbor boy, Cooper, one of MacLachlan's delightfully
well-adjusted youths, full of frank wisdom and a stabilizing influence. He is Horace, Margaret Mary, Emily Parmalee—the good
friend we would all like to have next door. Cooper notes that Cat
looks likes her mother in the pictures, but Cat turns to a picture of
her grandmother and declares: "There. That's who I look like!"
(15). Cat is, of course, rejecting her mother, and that troubles
Journey, who feels compelled to add, "You look like Mama, too"
(16). Here is the difference between the siblings and their handling of the crisis: Cat rejects her mother with almost icy indiffer-
ence, and Journey clings to a hopeless dream. Both are in a state
of denial, Cat denying that the abandonment matters and Journey
denying that it has happened.

And so the story moves quietly, occasionally with amusement. We see Journey driving to town so that Grandfather can take photographs from the car window. But it is not without protest: "I'm only a little boy," Journey pleads. "Then drive like a little boy," his grandfather retorts (22). Journey's reticence is the outward expression of his inward insecurity. He laments that a picture he took is no good—at least it is not perfect. But his grandfather admonishes, "What is perfect? Journey, a thing doesn't have to be perfect to be fine. That goes for a picture. That goes for life. . . . Things can be good enough" (29). It is at this point that Journey finally voices one of his deepest fears—that his mother left because he was not good enough. His grandfather firmly tells him that it was not his fault, but he understands at the same time that Journey cannot blame his mother. Then Journey recalls one of his earliest childhood memories: riding on his father's knee to the jingle "Trot, trot to Boston" and the image of a button on his father's shirt. "And," Journey continues, "he wouldn't let me fall. He and mama kept me safe and took care of me. . . ." (31). But the fond memories are soon swept away when he asks to see the pictures from his childhood, and his grandfather must tell him that "your mama tore them up" (32).

A stray cat comes to the farm and they name her Bloom, a name, like Journey's, out of medieval allegory, for Bloom is pregnant. And Bloom discovers the box of torn pictures under the bed in Journey's mother's old room. Journey then determines to paste them all together. The pile of shredded photographs is sharply contrasted with Cooper's home, a typical loving household filled with family pictures on the refrigerator, above the doorway, over the sideboard, and on the walls of the living room. (Cluttered homes are happy homes in MacLachlan's world.) When Journey tells Cooper's mother, Mrs. MacDougal, that his grandfather says "pictures show us the truth sometimes," she shows Journey a family portrait from her youth in which she, her parents, and her siblings appear to be the model family. What the picture does not show, she explains, is that her brother was, at the time, "pinching the devil out of me" (56). "Sometimes," she says, "the truth is somewhere behind the pictures. Not in them" (57).

There is an old movie, *Call Northside 777*, in which Jimmy
Stewart, a newspaper reporter, helps to secure a pardon for a
wrongly convicted man by proving that his accuser lied on the
witness stand. The irrefutable evidence comes from a photograph
enlarged several hundred times to reveal a key date on the mast-
head of a newspaper captured in the corner of the photograph. By
the same token, we are all aware of trick photography—of the
infamous sort that seems to verify the presence of ghosts, for
example, or the sophisticated computerized techniques that dazzle
us in the cinema. Photography is an elusive art. Sometimes it captures reality; sometimes it hides or distorts it. The photograph,
like all art forms, can be an ambiguous creation, and our response
to it depends upon what knowledge we bring to the experience. It
is experience that Journey must gain; like a Greek hero, he must
learn through suffering.

Upon his return from the MacDougals, Journey learns that
Bloom has had her kittens (giving new significance to her
name); but she gives birth in the box of torn photographs, eliminating any possibility, however remote, of Journey reassembling
the pieces. Journey takes the news with surprising aplomb, and
he insists on taking a group picture with the timer—so that he
can be in it as well. There follows a lyrical passage—in the present tense—describing the moments up to the clicking of the
shutter. It is a moment frozen in time—and key to Journey's
eventual understanding of things. In his haste to get himself
positioned in the picture, he tumbles across his grandfather's
lap, "and he holds me there, looking a little surprised, as if I'm a
newborn baby. I stare at the button on his shirt" (62). The experience triggers a vague image in the back of Journey's mind,
although he is still unable to complete the connection. It is the
image from the distant past when he rode on a man's knees
while the man sang "Trot, trot to Boston," and Journey was
attracted by a button on the man's shirt. The man, he had long
assumed, was his father; although clever readers may begin to
understand otherwise. The image of the newborn baby suggests
that this is the rebirth of Journey. It is a Journey who is more
self-assured, ready to let loose the past that had prevented him

from moving forward with his life. It is the turning point of the story.

Shortly after, Journey gets a telephone call from his mother—appropriately, there is faulty connection producing crackling on the line, symbolic of the difficulty of communication between mother and son. Journey's remarks are guarded; he clearly no longer feels the need to defend his mother or to protect her. He simply and straightforwardly says to his mother, "A cat has come . . . And the cat is a very good mother . . . And she is staying here with me. Forever" (64). That Journey has grown in understanding becomes clear when he relates this conversation to his grandfather. His mother invited him to come visit her, he explains, but Journey declined, "I told her I have a cat and kittens to take care of. . . . I told her someday, maybe; if she sent me words instead of money, I might visit. Maybe" (67). Journey later asks Cat if she hates their mother. She replies, "I hate what she did" (73). Journey agrees. This ability on the children's part to separate the person from the deed is a sign of maturity. And this recognition makes it easier for Journey to let go of the bitter memories of his past. Journey's letting go of this past, filled with its illusions about his parents, allows him to accept the present, including the great love his grandparents shower on him.

The final two chapters of the book take place some two months later. Grandmother plays her flute—music, as ever, soothing pain and adding to the beauty of the world—and Grandfather is engaged in some secretive enterprise in his "office" in the barn. Grandfather's office, it turns out, is a dark room where he has been making new prints from the negatives of the torn-up photographs. As Cat astutely observes to Journey, "Don't you know that Grandfather wants to give you back everything that Mama took away? He wants to give you family" (73). Among these pictures are photos of Journey's father, but to Journey's dismay he realizes that he does not remember his father's face—it does not look familiar. However, he immediately recognizes in another picture his grandfather, and he suddenly realizes that for all these years it had been his grandfather's face and the button on his grandfather's shirt that had remained so vividly and happily in his memory; it was on his grandfather's knees that he sat, and it was his grandfather who sang "Trot, trot to Boston" to him. This was the truth that Journey had been trying to remember—"It was *your* face," he says to his grandfather (82). And his grandfather points out to Journey the very moment when he realized this truth, the moment he tumbled into his grandfather's lap during the taking of the family photograph, and his grandfather shows him the evidence in the picture itself. It is nearly dawn when Journey and his grandfather "walk out of the barn, the night has gone, and the sun has come up" (83). Surely the implication is that the sun has arisen on a new and hopeful chapter in Journey's life.

Journey is a variation on a favorite MacLachlan theme, life's necessary losses and how to deal with them. MacLachlan makes effective use of the medium of photography to explore this theme. The wonderful ambivalence of photography, which can both reveal hidden depths of character and disguise or distort reality, serves well as a symbol of our memory.

Journey, the Screenplay

In 1995, MacLachlan wrote the screenplay for *Journey* for a Hallmark Hall of Fame television production. Since *Journey* was a longer book than *Sarah, Plain and Tall*, it required less embellishment and fewer structural changes to transform it into a two-hour film production. Much of the dialogue is taken word for word from the original text, but there are some significant additions.

Roles are created for a hired man, Boone, and his wife, Kate (who appears in a single scene). These characters serve as foils to Journey's grandparents, here named Marcus and Lottie, for Boone and Kate have lost their son Jody to death, whereas Marcus and Lottie have lost their daughter in another way. They also provide in the film the necessary adult interplay, presumably to broaden the audience appeal. Since both couples have, in one way or another, lost children, they share a common bond, but for the most part, very little comes of this character addition.

It is the expanded role of Min, Journey's mother, that is the most important change in the screenplay. Min (her name is changed from Liddie in the book) is seen at the beginning of the screenplay in a loud argument with her father—he pleads with her not to abandon her children, and she verbally lacerates him for being overbearing. Finally it is Marcus who says to her: "Don't come back this time, Min. It's not fair to Journey and Cat. You come and go . . . like a visitor. That's not a mother's way." Periodically throughout the script we see Min in a diner or a roadside cafe, always with a pay phone nearby. She calls her parents' home but hangs up without answering. Only at the end, as in the book, does she finally speak to Journey on the telephone. The screenplay, however, shows Min returning to the farm one last time to speak to her mother and to observe her children from afar—she does not go to them. In this interview with her mother, Min insists, "I can't live with Marcus, Mother. I can't. I'm sorry." Her mother simply nods in sympathetic understanding, and Min then gets into her car and drives off.

The expanded presence of Min and the explanation for her actions are likely to raise as many questions for the audience as they answer. The book leaves Liddie's motives deliberately ambiguous, although it suggests that she was a difficult child, one who always seemed to want to be somewhere else. The screenplay, on the other hand, places much of the blame for Min's actions rather decidedly on Marcus's shoulders, on his stubborn ways and his domineering demeanor. The problem with this explanation is that nothing else in Marcus's actions or words seems to indicate that he could be a parent so disagreeable as to drive his own daughter away. In fact, some viewers are likely to see just the opposite in Marcus. Journey's epiphany is that it was his grandfather who cared for him in his childhood; it was he who sang to him, he who was there for Journey when his own parents were not. That Marcus may be trying to compensate in his relationships with his grandchildren for his failures as a parent is not well supported either, since Min clearly refers to Marcus's headstrong ways in the present tense. Those familiar with the book may feel uneasy over the screenplay's shifting of the blame to Marcus, and they are likely to find the book's ambiguity over Liddie's relationship with her parents a more satisfactory approach.

The dialogue consists largely of staccato-like exchanges—frequently incomplete sentences, with the meaning contained in the silences or the expressive glances. The scenes tend to be brief—there are few intensive or lengthy interviews. The power of the imagery carries the significance—a typical technique of MacLachlan's. Her books and her screenplays are not talky. Pointless dialogue and empty scenes are not characteristic of her style. The sparse dialogue, on the other hand, increases the possibility for static scenes. In one respect, however, *Journey* is ideally suited to the screen because of its reliance on photography as a dominant image. Particularly effective are the use of the freeze-frame and the screen's ability to show us the photographs that the book must use words to describe. All this underscores the highly visual nature of MacLachlan's writing, her love of imagery and the richly suggestive quality it acquires in her hands.

Baby

One reviewer wrote of *Baby* (1993), "Is this a book for adults, young adults, or children? Hard to say, but it is one that will find its own audience, for it can neither be overlooked nor easily forgotten."[2] Indeed, *Baby* marks MacLachlan's continued development toward more serious and thought-provoking themes. It is another story of abandonment, but this time the interest is shifted from the abandoned child to the troubled family in whose care it is left. The narrator is Larkin, a girl of about 12 who lives with her father, whom she calls "Papa," her mother, "Mama," and her maternal grandmother, whom everyone affectionately calls "Byrd." Papa is a newspaper editor who drinks a little too much after work and furiously tap dances on the coffee table; Mama is an oil painter who too easily withdraws into her own world; and Byrd is a delightful eccentric who longs for something new and exciting. They live on a resort island off the New England coast, and as the book opens the summer season is drawing to a close and the tourists depart, returning the island to its few stalwart inhabitants. An inexplicable tension hangs over the first chapter, a secret sadness, a sense that the family's outward gaiety masks a lingering pain. We soon learn that the family's grief is for the death, a few months previously, of Larkin's baby brother, who lived only a day and was buried without a name in the island cemetery. The devastated family has not yet properly worked through its grief. It is after the last ferry leaves that they suddenly, without warning, encounter the thing that will alter their lives forever and perhaps even save them—a baby girl lying abandoned in a basket in their driveway.

Mama is ecstatic, but Papa is more guarded, a response justified by the note left in the basket: "This is Sophie. She is almost a year old and she is good." The note continues, "I cannot take care of her now, but I know she will be safe with you. . . . I will come back for her one day. I love her" (21–22). Larkin's response is jealousy, and it is only now that the reader is informed of the death of the baby boy. Larkin visits the grave marked with a tiny stone on which is inscribed simply, "Baby." As in Greek tragedy, death in MacLachlan's works always takes place off stage. MacLachlan is not interested in the process of dying itself; she is interested in the process of coping with loss. Larkin overhears her father pleading with her mother: "She is *not ours*. . . . Sophie is not a substitute" (35). And Larkin understands then and there that "someday she would go away. Another thing to miss" (36). Larkin and Papa attempt to remain detached to escape the pain of the inevitable loss. Mama cannot.

The story then relates the family's, indeed the whole island's, gradual acceptance of Sophie. Sophie is like a miraculous gift, spreading warmth and love through the innocence and purity of her nature. An almost unearthly being, she becomes the island's child. Through their experiences with Sophie, Larkin and her family eventually come to terms with their unspoken grief and are able to move on with their lives. *Baby* is an unusual story for MacLachlan in many ways. It takes place over the course of the school year, and a key role is played by a teacher/librarian, Ms. Minifred. Ms. Minifred, one of MacLachlan's wise and endearing eccentrics, is certainly a more admirable representative of her profession than Miss Barbizon in *The Facts and Fictions of Minna Pratt* (the only other MacLachlan novel set during the school year). She explains to the children that they will "be talking about the power of language . . . the power of words. And how words can change you." But Larkin is skeptical: "What about when there are no words? . . . *Silence can change you, too.* . . ." (42). She is, of course, thinking of the silence of her parents, their unwillingness or inability to speak of the death of her brother—even their refusal to name the baby as if that made him less real—and finally, of their failure to recognize that she, Larkin, carries the grief as well.

Larkin's best friend is Lalo Baldelli, whose parents own the local hotel. He is the strong, self-assured, comforter-confessor, a staple character in MacLachlan's novels. In many ways these characters serve as alter egos of the protagonists—Moira and Arthur, Margaret Mary and Cassie, and so on. Larkin envies Lalo for his ability to brave the perilous sea cliffs, whereas she timidly holds back. He is also alarmingly frank, another trait of these characters. When Larkin complains to Lalo that her brother was never named, he suggests that she name him. She responds, "What?" "You always do that," Lalo retorts. "You always say 'What?' when you don't know what to say. Or you don't want to answer. The fact is, if you need him named, then you name him" (54). We are reminded of Moira's sharp, sometimes brutal remarks to Arthur in *Arthur, for the Very First Time*, which serve to jar him out of his self-indulgent complacency. The truth is not always pleasant to hear. Lalo is the character who holds up the mirror to Larkin's face—in other words, he is the best of friends. It is only now that Larkin is beginning to make an important connection: *"I don't know how to love Sophie because I don't know how to love my brother"* (55). The feelings are inextricably interwoven.

Like all of MacLachlan's books, *Baby* is a book about love. And MacLachlan shows us that love is found in some of the most unexpected places. For example, there is Ms. Minifred, who is in so many ways the classic, stereotypical schoolmarm, ecstatic over "wondrous words." To Larkin's surprise, she learns that Ms. Minifred is in love with the school janitor, an unconventional character nicknamed Rebel who rides a Harley-Davidson motorcycle and sports a leather jacket, spiked hair, and a tattoo that says

"Wild Eunice." Eunice turns out to be, of course, Ms. Minifred. Their mutual affection (the last time Ms. Minifred is mentioned in the book, she is riding off on Rebel's motorcycle) demonstrates the multifaceted nature of love, and their wonderful eccentricity immensely enriches the world. Lalo's mother and father provide yet another example of love—and eccentricity. His mother, Marvella Baldelli, possesses old-world charm. She fears electricity, for instance, believing that it lurks in the light sockets waiting to leap onto anyone who gets too near. She also believes that "germs cannot penetrate wool," so she wraps Lalo up "like a mummy." She is tall, beautiful, and terrified of the water. Yet she insists on living on an island because of her love for her husband, a fisherman turned hotel operator.

Larkin is surrounded by love, and she suddenly realizes that she loves Sophie, almost in spite of herself, when one day Sophie reaches out for Larkin. At that moment Larkin thinks: *"There are no words for this"* (63). This sentiment echoes that of Sarah Wheaton's brother, who believes that sometimes during a storm there is a color in the sea for which there are no words. Language is not always adequate to convey extraordinary beauty or the depth of feeling found in the human heart. But it is, in fact, through language that Larkin finds the means to bring closure to her grief and to restore her own peace of mind. In school, Ms. Minifred tells the class of her brother, William, who died young and of the difficulty she had facing his death. She reads Edna St. Vincent Millay's "Dirge without Music"—a poem important to her brother and one that gave her comfort because "it said what I felt" (85). The poem is included in its entirety, and the following stanza also serves as a prologue to the book:

I am not resigned to the shutting away of loving hearts in the hard
    ground.
So it is, and so it will be, for so it has been, time out of mind:
Into the darkness they go, the wise and the lovely. Crowned
With lilies and with laurel they go; but I am not resigned.

These words give Larkin the courage to confront her mother and to bare her feelings about her dead brother: "I never saw the baby! . . . And you never named him! . . . And you never talked to me about him!" (90). Mama then shares with Larkin the painting she has been working on for so long, the one that has kept her shut away from the family—it is a painting of the dead baby. This marks the turning point of the story, for it is now that Larkin can freely confess her love for Sophie without feeling guilty about not having had the chance to love her brother. The "power of language" has enabled Larkin, as Ms. Minifred told her it could, to face her feelings, to express her grief, and to shed the burden of her sorrow after so many months of silence.

Over the course of the story, which covers nearly a year, Sophie learns to walk and to talk and to love her new family. Sophie's growing vocabulary (she learns "dammit" from Lalo's father while he is wrestling with the Christmas decorations) prompts a discussion between Larkin and her father. Papa says with regret, "You grew up almost without me noticing" (96). When Papa says to Larkin, "I love you, Lark," Sophie responds, "Love" (97). Sophie's growing vocabulary parallels the family's increasing ability to verbalize their feelings.

With spring comes the inevitable. On their return from their first beach outing, the family sees Sophie's mother on their porch. We cannot help noticing the inverted symbolism MacLachlan uses with the seasons. The death of the baby had come in the spring preceding the opening of the book. Hope, in the form of baby Sophie, comes with the approach of fall, and Larkin confesses her love for Sophie sometime in the winter. With the spring, potential despair arrives once again with the coming of Sophie's mother to take Sophie away. Her mother has been like a phantom. Careful readers will have noted her silent presence in chapter 2—"A young woman holding a baby stood near, watching us" (14). Of course, only in retrospect do we realize who she is. Her brief letters arrive regularly throughout the year, some containing money, one a small gift at Christmas, annoying reminders to Larkin and her family that Sophie is only a temporary visitor in their home. And at the spring picnic on the beach, in the midst of the crisp beauty of a New England spring with the family frolicking happily in the sand, MacLachlan inserts these two lines: "Far away, cormorants flew close to the water in a line. Behind them the ferry moved slowly toward us" (107). It is the ferry carrying Sophie's mother. As in Brueghel's painting of the fall of Icarus, MacLachlan's seemingly frivolous details carry a heavy weight. The book has been described as sparse—but each of those sparse details is significant and not a word is lost.

The book's one weakness may be Sophie's mother's excuse for her abandonment—Sophie's father was sick and needed an operation, and his recuperation would require all of her mother's time. Quite likely MacLachlan wished to assure the reader that Sophie would be in equally good hands when she returned to her mother, and in any event, Sophie's fate is not the crux of this story. Once Sophie and her mother leave, Byrd finally takes charge and informs the family that they are going to talk: "You cannot walk away and leave this behind as if it never happened. . . . Like the baby" (121). Byrd insists on "words." "Even Sophie had words," Larkin tells them (122). And then Papa tenderly whispers to Mama: "Words, Lily, . . . Not painting. Not dancing. *Words*" (122). Mama then describes the baby's appearance, speaking about him for the first time. And then and there, they name the baby William. We conquer our fears by naming them—and by naming the dead baby, Larkin and her parents are able to face the fact of his death. They hold a funeral service at the graveside, where "WILLIAM" has been engraved on the headstone. And there at last they are able to say good-bye.

The story closes in the summer 10 years later, when Larkin is returning to the island for her grandmother Byrd's funeral. On the ferry to the island she meets Sophie, now a young girl, and her mother, returning also to attend the funeral. It is Sophie's first visit since she left with her mother 10 years before. Larkin and Sophie reminisce and Sophie recalls deep-seated memories of her year with Larkin's family—a good year for them all. This closing chapter frames the story and draws attention to the storytelling device—a technique MacLachlan is fond of using. It seems especially significant in this book, which takes as its theme the impor-

tance of sharing our stories, the power of language. Brief interludes that signify Sophie's memories as a baby are placed rather
sporadically between chapters. These constitute a narrative shift;
they are recollections of an older Sophie—but related in the third
person. Each passage serves to highlight imagery that will become
important in the succeeding narrative—hands, the color red, the
clouds, and the sound of voices making words. These passages
effectively convey the random nature of a child's earliest memories. And so Sophie's disjunctive thoughts are interwoven with
Larkin's chronological narrative to produce a unified whole, the
book closing with a coda depicting Sophie and Larkin reunited at
Byrd's funeral. Structurally, *Baby* is one of MacLachlan's most
carefully honed works.

   Baby is the most poignant of MacLachlan's books. She has said
that she wrote *Baby* because she "had no more babies," her own
children having grown up and left home.[3] She, who had so thoroughly enjoyed motherhood, was suddenly bereft of her children
and facing the empty nest. The grief of Larkin's parents was her
own inward sorrow and that of all parents whose babies grow up
and leave them. This book was MacLachlan's way of dealing with
this separation in her life, her way of coming to terms with these
necessary losses. It is also very likely that in Byrd's death and
funeral we find the author's farewell to her own mother who had
died of Alzheimer's disease some years before. MacLachlan's
mother had always played an important role in her life. A generous and loving woman, she served as MacLachlan's own model for
motherhood and provided MacLachlan with the inspiration for
Aunt Elda, and quite probably all of MacLachlan's "unclaimed
treasures" to one degree or another. If *Baby* is a work of great
power, it is because it was written with passion felt deeply and
personally by the author. It is an exquisite expression of human
compassion, the acceptance of loss, and faith in the ever turning
circle of life.

Chapter Six
The Art of Patricia MacLachlan

Tell them I sing.

—Sarah, Plain and Tall

It is always risky to assess a living and working author—a task much like hitting the proverbial moving target. It is especially difficult in the case of Patricia MacLachlan, since her more recent works have exhibited some decidedly new directions. Nevertheless, some distinctive threads running through her work permit a few general observations.

Landscapes and Interiors

As her picture book *All the Places to Love* so beautifully reveals, the writer's landscape is a significant and moving influence for MacLachlan. Her writings are anchored by the rural West of her formative years and the rural New England of her later childhood and adulthood. The settings of many of her books are an interesting amalgam of these two geographic regions. The typical MacLachlan story takes place in a rural area in the vague, not-too-distant past (the historical novels excepted, of course). Dates and places are deliberately obscured to give the stories a greater universality and a more lasting appeal. Adult readers may recognize in many of the books something of the aura of the 1950s (give or take a decade)—or rather, the 1950s as they appear in the popular imagination as well as in the increasingly clouded memories of those of us who experienced them. The books portray a time that is somehow quieter, slower paced, more closely in touch with the simple things of life. External forces never intrude—as they seldom do in childhood. No one mentions world affairs; there are few points of reference that would pinpoint the time. Television is notably absent from most of the novels, as are such modern conveniences as microwave ovens, personal computers, and videocassette recorders. In *Arthur, for the Very First Time*, we see a peddler selling his wares from a donkey cart, certainly something from another era. In fact, MacLachlan's characters seem to walk more than they drive, and when they do drive, it is a curiously comical activity. Old Pepper in *Unclaimed Treasures* and Twig in *The Facts and Fictions of Minna Pratt* are both abominable drivers, and 11-year-old Journey is forced to drive his grandfather's car, which is so old it has a running board, while his grandfather sits in the back and takes candid shots of the surrounding countryside. Driving is treated in these books almost as something out of the ordinary.

The geographical location in MacLachlan's novels is equally misty. No towns are named (or states), and MacLachlan's characters seldom travel far from home. The worlds portrayed are fairly closed worlds, perhaps intentionally to focus the stories on the interior lives of the characters. Although *Baby* is the only book that is actually set on an island, most of the novels exhibit a similar sense of isolation. MacLachlan's heart is in the country, which increases the sense of isolation and enhances the romanticism—only one novel takes place in a city, *The Facts and Fictions of Minna Pratt*, and that is a remarkably idyllic city. There is a strong hint of New England in some of the novels, especially in *Cassie Binegar* and *Baby*, and *Sarah, Plain and Tall* and *Skylark* are set on the Western prairie and in Maine. But for the most part, the stories could take place almost anywhere. Certainly Minna Pratt could be taking her cello lessons in virtually any city in America, and Uncle Wrisby and Aunt Elda's farm could as well be in the Midwest as in the East. Again, the geographic location is not as important as the feeling the place exudes—the simple life, held close to the earth and untrammeled by the bustle of modern urban living. It is a world where values are clearer, where life is reduced to the fundamentals.

Although MacLachlan's landscapes are important in establishing mood, they never present challenges to her characters, nor do they help to define character. Rather, they are scenic backdrops against which the protagonist's inner life may be examined. Her novels portray an almost pastoral world filled with people engaged in happy pursuits and generally oblivious to the twentieth century. But she will not forbear from placing the serpent into her paradise. Hers is not a world of idle shepherds pining for their loves but of flesh-and-blood children suffering as we all have on the road to self-discovery and self-actualization.

If landscapes are important in establishing the milieu of a MacLachlan book, it is the psychological interior of the characters that is the most engaging aspect. The typical MacLachlan novel takes as its protagonist a child of about 12, introspective and precocious but troubled over certain rather natural changes that are taking place in his or her life. Although the majority of her protagonists are female, and it is easy to apply feminist criticism to much of her work[1], MacLachlan is a writer of broad sensitivity with the ability to create tender males as well as tough females. Masculinity and femininity are only biological facts in MacLachlan's books, and her male and female characters are faced with quite similar problems. Her protagonists are often aspiring writers, which makes them introspective and observant. By the same token, they tend to be self-absorbed and egocentric, and the great challenge for them is to see the world as others see it. In *Cassie Binegar* we find a striking image of the child's self-absorption when Cassie tries to see the moon over the water at night, but "her own face was in the way" (17). How well MacLachlan comprehends the minds of preadolescents whose vision of the world is often obstructed by their own image. It is this interior life that interests her and is the reason for the reflection and introspection that prompt reviewers to describe her books as "gentle," "tender," and "quietly beautiful." MacLachlan eschews intense dramatic action and focuses our attention on the psychological underpinnings of the protagonist; it is a quieter process but one that offers exceedingly rich rewards.

A stock character in MacLachlan's novels is the wise friend—sometimes a sibling (Willa's brother, McGrew, or Minna's brother, Nicholas)—who is the confidant, support, and stay for the protagonist. This character is self-assured, frank, and usually unemotional (but sensitive nevertheless), and he or she serves as a touchstone to reality for the protagonist. Arthur's friend Moira, Cassie Binegar's friend Mary Margaret, and Larkin's friend Lalo are all bold, outspoken individuals, solid and less complex than the protagonist but interesting nonetheless. (It is interesting to note how often in MacLachlan's novels the confidante is of the opposite sex.) Occasionally this character will be the subject of a subplot—such as with Moira and her grandfather in *Arthur, for the Very First Time*. Often these characters provide comic relief, which in itself can be a form of staying in touch with reality. However, they are never mere sidekicks but penetrating personalities who are unafraid of telling the protagonists what they need to hear or holding a mirror up to their faces and forcing them to take a long hard look.

Typically there is at least one elderly character—a grandparent or an older neighbor—who also functions as a wise counselor. These characters are always lively, usually delightfully eccentric, and much loved. It is no accident that much of the wise advice in MacLachlan's books comes from either the young or the old—it only infrequently comes from parents. MacLachlan believes that it is from the young and the old that we get the keenest observations and the most honest and direct responses. Her treatment of the old is a refreshing departure from much of mainstream children's literature. The elderly in children's stories have not always been happily portrayed, and the formidable, crotchety spinster has been an unfortunate staple at least as far back as Aunt March in *Little Women*. The figure of the elder who is to be respected but kept at a distance from children has been one of the great disservices perpetrated by too many children's books. Just as MacLachlan has consciously attempted to break down the gender barriers in her character portraits, she has taken aim at the disconcerting and even cruel stereotypes of the old.

It could be argued that MacLachlan is perpetuating another stereotype in portraying her old people as eccentrics, but this charge can be quickly countered by pointing to the many eccentric characters of all ages throughout her stories. Many of her supporting characters have endearing but peculiar traits—an uncle who speaks in rhyme, a cousin who dresses in feathers, an island wife who fears electricity and hates the water, a sage street musician, and a young violinist burgeoning with useless information. These individuals provide the source of much of MacLachlan's humor, a potent antidote to the potentially serious psychological trauma through which the protagonist is working. Her characters are in love with life and fiercely independent thinkers who will not be stifled by empty social mores. MacLachlan's goal seems to be the rejection of all stereotypes and the encouragement of self-confidence and individualism.

Perhaps another stereotype she has attempted to dismantle is that of the jealous sibling. As suggested above, siblings in MacLachlan's books are supportive and caring. Most of her early books were about only children (*The Sick Day; Through Grandpa's Eyes; Moon, Stars, Frogs, and Friends; Mama One, Mama Two; and Tomorrow's Wizard*). But beginning with *Cassie Binegar* (Cassie's brothers play supportive if relatively minor roles) and *Seven Kisses in a Row*, MacLachlan has created a series of books celebrating the joys of sibling relationships. Perhaps MacLachlan, an only child, is creating the childhood she never knew but always wished for, or perhaps she is recreating the happy relationships of her own children; more likely, it is a little bit of both. Like her own, MacLachlan's fictional families are small—only two protagonists, Cassie Binegar and Willa Pinkerton, have more than one sibling. But in her later and longer works, none of her protagonists is technically an only child (in Arthur's case his sibling is unborn, and in Larkin's case her sibling has died). It is also interesting that her siblings tend to be of the opposite sex and that she has never written a book about sisters—it may be a subject that is beyond her ken or simply beyond her interest.

It is not only that MacLachlan does not write about sibling rivalry; in fact, she seldom writes about any sort of interpersonal conflict. When such a conflict does exist, it is typically between parent and child (usually an extraordinarily one-sided conflict as that between Cassie Binegar or Minna Pratt and their mothers). In addition to Minna and Cassie, Arthur, Willa, Journey, and Larkin all have grievances against their parents—and except in Journey's case, most are not particularly well-founded. In fact, parents—at least those who have not abandoned their children—

are actually quite favorably portrayed by MacLachlan. This vision of parenthood is likely derived from MacLachlan's own experiences and inevitably opens her up to the criticism of romanticizing the family. Such a criticism will seem absurd to anyone who has carefully read the body of her work. Her families are not unqualifiedly happy—she is no latter-day Margaret Sidney. Her children can be irascible and her parents distant, maddening silences reach across her pages as communication fails, and we see remarkably few signs of physical affection between parent and child. In other words, her works on this count are remarkably realistic.

Cassie Binegar laments of her family, "Why can't we be like everyone else?" (*Cassie Binegar,* 16). It is the typical complaint of a child her age, beset by peer pressure and the psychological need to fit in. Her conflicts are internal ones, reflecting the turbulent psyche of the preteen-ager. MacLachlan writes about that time in life when the fledgling is perched precariously on the edge of the nest, surveying the wide world around and feeling at once thrilled at the distant prospect and desperately alone. It is the time when the parents must be ready to make a quick rescue if necessary but must also refrain from preventing the fledgling's flight (or from pushing).

Language and Communication

Cassie Binegar remarks to Jason, the writer with whom she is infatuated, "Why is it . . . that I like to hear what you say even though I don't understand what you're saying at all" (*Cassie Binegar,* 79). The limitations of language are a recurrent theme in MacLachlan's work, exemplified by Uncle Wrisby's stubborn, old-fashioned precept of not believing "anything written. Only what I see" (*Arthur,* 14); the observation of Sarah's brother that sometimes the sea is a color for which there is no word; and Minna Pratt's exasperation with her mother, who "asks the wrong questions [and] answers with the wrong answers" (*Facts and Fictions,* 67). If this seems an unusual preoccupation for a writer, we may rightly ask, "Who better to understand both the strengths and weaknesses of language?"

In many of her books, beginning with the simple wordplay found in *The Sick Day*, MacLachlan explores the use of language. She reiterates the sentiment that language is sometimes inadequate to communicate feelings—yet, ironically, only language can relate that sentiment. MacLachlan's ambiguous messages about language may perfectly capture the confusion of many 11- and 12-year-olds beset by strange new and unsettling emotions for which they have no adequate point of reference or vocabulary. The young teen's desperate plea "My parents don't understand me" is, in large degree, a cry of helplessness over not being able to articulate the frustrations and tribulations of childhood and adolescence.

The metafictional devices used in *Cassie Binegar* and *Unclaimed Treasures* have already been discussed, but worth mentioning again is the effect of these devices to keep us cognizant of the story-telling process. It is this process that is so important in the healing of ruptures, the assuagement of losses. MacLachlan includes nearly as many storytellers in her books as she does other artists— they are parents, foster parents, grandparents, great aunts, neighbors, and friends. The storytelling process naturally validates MacLachlan's profession as a writer, and it is a simple leap to suggest that her husband's profession as a psychologist has significantly influenced her belief in the therapeutic value of shared experiences and feelings.

In *The Facts and Fictions of Minna Pratt*, Minna, who spends so much of her time being frustrated by her mother's apparent failure to communicate with her—asking the wrong questions, answering with the wrong answers—learns that talking, even if it seems pointless or misdirected, is far better than the silence practiced by the proper but out-of-touch Mrs. Ellerby. It is noteworthy that so many of MacLachlan's characters are writers or budding writers—Arthur, Cassie Binegar (and Jason), Willa's father, Anna Witting, and Minna's mother. MacLachlan is exploring the limits of language, the writer's need to write, and perhaps, our need to hear stories. Her characters frequently, and usually incorrectly, believe that there are things best left unspoken, as if the silence will negate them. Arthur leaves his parents' letters unopened, creating a silence between him and his parents with the clear implication that this will halt the unpleasant changes Arthur believes to be taking place. His Uncle Wrisby acts similarly when he does not want to know what dangers might befall his pregnant sow if not properly cared for. Aunt Elda says, "He figures that if he doesn't know about it . . . that maybe it won't happen at all" (*Arthur*, 59). In *Journey* we find the heartbreaking silence of Journey's mother, who sends money but no words in her envelopes. Whether it is Cassie Binegar's unspoken feeling of guilt or the silent pain of Larkin and her parents, the things left unsaid are the source of considerable anguish.

Another noteworthy aspect of MacLachlan's use of language is its decided poetic quality. MacLachlan, who has published no poetry, composes novels that in their sparsity of language, evocative word imagery, reflective silences, and mellifluous rhythms bear much in common with poetry. One of the great achievements in *Sarah, Plain and Tall* is the effective use of sea and prairie imagery—one representing Sarah and one the Wittings—at first so apparently different, but at last, as the images are gracefully interwoven, so quite obviously alike. By the story's close, the union between Sarah and the Wittings seems both fitting and natural. The evocative language, relying heavily on the visual symbol, has become a mainstay of a MacLachlan novel. Like the crisp language of the folktale, MacLachlan's works are rife with concrete imagery—the binoculars and the prism in *Arthur, for the Very First Time*, the huge patterned tablecloth and the space it creates in *Cassie Binegar*, the various artistic references (discussed in more detail later) in virtually every book. Indeed, the comparison with folktales is an appropriate one, for MacLachlan reads all her work aloud, as the folktale is intended, to listen for the rhythm of the language and to weigh its sound.

Willa Cather, herself a fine stylist, wrote of Sarah Orne Jewett's art, "It is so tightly yet so lightly built, so little encumbered with heavy materialism that deteriorates and grows old-fashioned."[2] Much the same can be said of MacLachlan's style, which has been reduced to its essence, all extraneous matter removed. Like the poet's, her language is distilled, and every word is to be read and savored.

Art and Life

One of the great underlying themes in MacLachlan's work is the significance of art in its myriad forms. Virtually every book she has written—including the picture books—pays homage to some art form: drawing, painting, music, photography, dance, or writing. Of course, the impetus comes from her own intense experience with art—as an amateur musician (amateur in the purist sense of the word: a "lover") and as a professional writer. Yet the persistence with which she writes about art suggests a deep conviction that art is more than aesthetic pleasure or decoration. For MacLachlan, art holds important keys to a fulfilling life experience. Art can give us an alternative way of seeing things as well as a means of expressing what we feel.

Susanne Langer defines art as "the creation of perceptible forms of expressive human feeling"[3] and claims that the "aim of art is insight, understanding of the essential feeling of life."[4] If we accept this explanation we have come a long way toward understanding the role of art in MacLachlan's books. Her characters long for insight, for understanding. Her protagonists suffer the agonies of coming of age, they no longer understand their parents (if they ever did), they are anticipating the mysteries of first love, and they are experiencing the pain of separation and loss. Her protagonists—wary and uncertain of what they know or feel—are passive observers, contemplating the business of life going on about them, seeking to make sense of it all. In short, they are ideally suited to be artists. On the surface, little happens in a MacLachlan book, and a reader looking for a heart-stopping adventure would do well to look elsewhere. But just beneath the calm of the leisurely paced plot is an emotional turbulence that sensitive readers will find both compelling and familiar.

The episodic structure of her works—even evidenced in her picture books—is ideally suited to MacLachlan's method of character exploration and delineation. It also reinforces the sense of community that is so important in her books. Describing the narratives of many of the notable children's writers, one critic notes that "they tend to be episodic, built primarily around the continuous small-scale negotiations and daily procedures through which communities sustain themselves."[5] Whether or not the episodic plot is a feminine literary trait, as some commentators maintain, or simply the narrative pattern best suited to the domestic story (which women seem more likely to write) is not the pertinent issue here. MacLachlan's subject matter and thematic concerns are most effectively approached through the episodic pattern, in which the details of everyday living are revealed as natural and integral parts of a symbiotic community.

At the same time, the episodic structure of her works demands that strong unifying threads tie the disparate elements together. Art is often that thread. Music is the most pervasive art form in MacLachlan's books, probably because of her own personal interest in music. However, another very legitimate reason for using music exists. One critic has noted that "writers of some of the most enduring children's books characterize and affirm community through collaborative musical performance."[6] And Jan Susina has argued that music plays an important metaphorical role in Wilder's *Little House on the Prairie* in linking the settlers with the prairie and making them a part of that landscape and in sustaining the family's spirit through their adventures in that rugged terrain.[7] Music in our lives is often part of a communal activity. Even when only one person is performing the music, all those within earshot become participants (albeit sometimes unwillingly, as I recall our neighbor's early morning tuba practices). The "Unclaimed Treasures" attempt to play a Beethoven trio, but they miss their third party, Horace's mother, and her absence prevents the music from being complete. The special relationship between music and the musician is beautifully portrayed in *The Facts and Fictions of Minna Pratt* when the members of the quartet are forced to play the Mozart piece while they face opposite corners. This emphasizes the importance of each individual, who must perfect his or her technique and who must be aware of his or her performance, yet the individual notes continue to blend into a single and, it is hoped, harmonious body of sound. It is an exquisite metaphor for the individual's role in the community and the community's effect on the individual. Music further signifies the harmony of the community in *Journey* when Journey's mother, upon abandoning her children, leaves behind her flute. Journey's grandmother picks up this emblem of her daughter's rejection of her role in the community and begins to learn to play it herself. As she improves, so does her relationship with Journey.

The role of the artist in MacLachlan's books is multifaceted. The artist is intuitive, feeling things more deeply than most people. The artist is also a seer, seeing things in ways we do not see them. And perhaps most importantly, the artist is a communicator, a spokesperson, whose gift is the ability to share those feelings and visions with the community (a reminder of the singular derivation of "communicate" and "community"). The artist's work is largely metaphorical, a visual or auditory representation of abstract feelings. And metaphor becomes necessary when language fails. MacLachlan's references to the limitations of language—colors for which there are no words, words whose meanings we do not comprehend—remind us once again of Langer, who writes: "Artistic expression abstracts aspects of the life of feeling which have no names, which have to be presented to sense and intuition rather than to a word-bound, note-taking consciousness."[8] MacLachlan rejects the notion of art for art's sake. Art for her has a moral dimension and a utilitarian purpose in addition to its aesthetic value. In *Arthur, for the Very First Time,* Aunt Elda reads Randall Jarrell's poem, "The Mockingbird," which concludes: "He imitates the world he drove away / So well that for a minute, in the moonlight, / Which one's the mockingbird? which one's the world?" (*Arthur,* 23). Art and life are inextricably interwoven. Art validates our sense of community, and the community informs the artistic creation. For the creators, art is important because it provides a means of self-expression; for the observers, it is important because it provides alternative ways of interpreting the world and thus broadens our vision; for everyone, it is important because it reaffirms our humanity and our communal spirit.

Separations and Gains

MacLachlan has said that she sees life as a series of separations and gains, and that theme is pervasive in her writing, even in her early picture books. The fantasy *Moon, Stars, Frogs, and Friends* is the story of a prince transformed into a frog, losing his true love in the process. It is also the story of a lonely frog who happily befriends a prince. Together they learn the value of friendship and of family; they turn their mutual losses into gains as the prince is eventually returned to his true love, the frog finds his life's companion, and they all end up fast friends. In *Mama One, Mama Two*, MacLachlan turns to a more serious form of separation—that of parent from child (an idea that, as we have seen, lingers as a compelling shadow in her writings). *Mama One, Mama Two* is more characteristic of MacLachlan than *Moon, Stars, Frogs, and Friends*, partly because it deals with human beings in real-life situations and partly because it offers no easy solutions to life's problems. Maudie's mother may eventually return from the psychiatric care in which she has been placed—but it will not happen between the covers of this book. In the meantime, Maudie must learn to cope with the separation, which she does by engaging in the storytelling process and by talking about her circumstances and her feelings. In the process, she is assisted by understanding friends, her foster mother, and a psychologist. *Tomorrow's Wizard* also deals with separation—or more precisely, the preparation for separation—as the apprentice wizard Murdoch decides to depart from his wise and kindly mentor, Tomorrow, to be transformed into a mortal. The subsequent melancholy that Tomorrow experiences over the loss of his young friend gives the ending its bittersweet quality.

"Bittersweet" is a term MacLachlan has used to describe her writings in general—an accurate assessment. Her works are bittersweet because they deal with the "necessary losses" of life, to use Judith Viorst's popularized phrase. In her book of that title, Viorst writes:

> When we think of loss we think of the loss, through death, of the people we love. But loss is a far more encompassing theme in our

life. For we lose not only through death, but also by leaving and being left, by changing and letting go and moving on. And our losses include not only our separations and departures from those we love, but our conscious and unconscious losses of romantic dreams, impossible expectations, illusions of freedom and power, illusions of safety—and the loss of our own younger self, the self that thought it always would be unwrinkled and invulnerable and immortal.[9]

MacLachlan treats necessary losses in *Arthur, for the Very First Time*; Arthur is losing his privileged role as the only child and his friend Moira has lost her parents and is in danger of losing her grandfather. We find it also in *Cassie Binegar* with Cassie who has lost her grandfather to death; in *Unclaimed Treasures* with Horace whose mother has temporarily abandoned the family and with Willa who must give up her imagined romance with Horace's father; in *Sarah, Plain and Tall* with Anna and Caleb who have lost their mother and with Sarah who must give up her comfortable life by the sea to accept new challenges; and in *Journey* with a mother's willing abandonment of her two children. Of course, *Baby* is a book entirely about losses. First is the loss through death of Larkin's baby brother, then Sophie's loss of her mother through temporary abandonment, and the loss of Sophie to Larkin's family when the child's mother returns. Finally there is the loss, also through death, of Byrd. With each loss, Larkin and her family are forced to grow—for as a result of separation we must reach out in new directions, discover strengths we were not before required to use. Larkin draws her inspiration in part from Edna St. Vincent Millay's "Dirge Without Music," which insists, "I am not resigned to the shutting away of loving hearts in the hard ground." The line both validates the anger we feel toward death and our stubborn resistance in the face of death. We are reminded of Dylan Thomas's defiant "Do not go gentle in that good night." But there are also important things that separations—even death—cannot take from us: the memories and the love.

MacLachlan never suggests that healing is a simple process. Her characters typically begin by trying to work through their pain alone. They are often maddeningly silent, introspective to a fault. In all cases, the assuagement for the loss comes in large part from the characters articulating their feelings—sharing their fears, their pain, and their anxieties with one another. Occasionally it takes a strong and sensible character like Grandma Byrd in *Baby* to insist, "We are going to talk now" (120). Sometimes, as in *Cassie Binegar*, the healing comes as the gradual result of a series of tangentially related events, all of which illumine the character's understanding. The subtitle of Viorst's book is "The Loves, Illusions, Dependences and Impossible Expectations That All of Us Have to Give Up in Order to Grow." It can be said with little exaggeration that this is the dominant theme of MacLachlan's writing.

Continuity and Change

Related to this notion of necessary losses, or perhaps another way of looking at those losses, is the concept of life's cyclical nature and the inevitability of change in the face of humanity's seemingly natural resistance to change and its desire for stability and continuity. Consider how many of MacLachlan's characters lament the changes being wrought in their lives. Arthur resents the new baby that is about to clutter up his life and potentially displace him. Emma in *Seven Kisses in a Row* is disturbed by the change caused in her everyday routine by the arrival of her aunt and uncle. And, in one of the clearest expressions of this resistance to change, Cassie Binegar refuses to accept her grandfather's death, deplores the clutter and confusion of her home life, and longs for the orderly, if superficial, life led by the family of her close friend Margaret Mary. It is Margaret Mary who detests the plastic plants with which her mother decorates their immaculate house; she much prefers the marigolds because "they grow . . . and they'll change. New blooms. They won't always be the same" (*Cassie Binegar,* 94). MacLachlan's stories keep reminding us that things will not always be the same. The changes are sometimes quite sobering and may initially be unhappy ones. Families are broken up (Moira's in *Arthur, for the Very First Time,* Journey and Cat's in *Jour-*

ney, and Sophie's in *Baby*), people die (Papa in *Cassie Binegar* and Anna and Caleb's mother in *Sarah, Plain and Tall*), and the forces of nature work against us (the drought in *Skylark*). Positive changes also occur, although we may not always recognize them as such at first. Most prominent among this sort of change is the birth of a baby, a common occurrence in MacLachlan's writing. Birth is of course a new beginning, and in many ways our lives are made up of great chapters framed by closures and new beginnings (much like the wonderfully structured narrative in *Unclaimed Treasures* that begins with a funeral and ends with a birth—a narrative embedded in a larger framework, a story within a story, that reinforces the cyclical nature of life).

MacLachlan's works are quite devoid of religious implications. Organized religion and deities are seldom mentioned. Only Aunt Elda, in *Arthur, for the Very First Time*, is portrayed as a churchgoer, but in deliberate contrast, Uncle Wrisby is completely indifferent to religion, sleeps through the church services, and grumbles about the requisite offering. MacLachlan's artists are not divinely inspired, nor are they vehicles through which deities speak. The prospect of an afterlife is never mentioned as a comfort for the bereaved (nor is it denied; it simply is not an issue). Instead, nature and the wonders of life's regeneration are the spiritual forces that move her characters. A form of secular humanism pervades MacLachlan's writing; the faith of her characters is in the human spirit, and they find their strength in their common humanity. The absence of a religious dimension from MacLachlan's work often goes unnoticed because of her generally positive, hopeful outlook. And the omission of religion is quite likely part of her deliberate effort at writing an inclusive literature, embracing a wide variety of personal beliefs.

As has been made patently obvious by this time, MacLachlan, more than most authors, writes out of what she has lived and observed. But she also once remarked that "you write not about what you know, but about what you care passionately for."[10] She is passionate about people and celebrates the strength that lies beneath their deceptively fragile facades. She is passionate about human relationships and what we all can offer one another. She is passionate about life and sees beauty in its marvelous complexity and stunning patterns. One critic has written that "humankind cannot bear very much abstraction or discursive reasoning. The stories of our days and the stories in our days are joined in that autobiography we are all engaged in making and remaking, as long as we live, which we never complete, though we all know how it is going to end."[11] This describes MacLachlan's inspiration. The characters and episodes she creates are drawn from a storehouse of memories filled through many years of patient observation and listening. *She* is Cassie Binegar under that table draped with the huge tablecloth; *her* husband is the father in *The Sick Day*; *she* is Minna Pratt's mother; *her* daughter is Minna Pratt; *her* father is Uncle Wrisby, and it is *his* garden of roses and radishes, and he is also Old Pepper in *Unclaimed Treasures*, exuberant, outspoken, forever young. But from these very personal expressions, MacLachlan is able to create stories filled with universal truths speaking to all of us. She has made *her* stories *our* stories.

Influence and Assessment

Patricia MacLachlan is still too new on the literary scene to have influenced other writers of note. However, the distinctiveness of her style and the increasing fame that is likely to result from the television adaptations of her works make it inevitable that she will have imitators. Certainly, a budding writer of children's books could hardly choose a better stylist from whom to learn the craft. And the general caliber of television programming would be significantly elevated if more screenwriters would emulate MacLachlan's work for that medium.

Reviewers have used such epithets as "a worthy successor to Wilder's Little House books" (written of *Sarah, Plain and Tall*),[12] "warm, affectionate view of life,"[13] "graceful language and an uncommon depth of understanding."[14] Her books have been praised as tender, her characters as wonderfully eccentric, and her language as resonant and lucid. Of *Baby*, one reviewer wrote, "It is difficult to read her sentences only once, and even more difficult to part from her novel."[15] Her continued growth and development as a writer and her exploration of some of the more somber aspects of life have kept her writing fresh and vibrant. Craig Virden, her first agent, longtime friend, and sometime editor, has observed her development over the years. He notes that her writing has always been "very internal, very cerebral."[16] Virden is also quite accurate when he says that her writing over the years has gotten even more deeply personal and "more profound."

MacLachlan is a romantic writer. Her view of the world is of a place that is fundamentally good, filled with people fundamentally loving and generous and tolerant, living lives that are fundamentally rich and rewarding, but not without pain, suffering, or cost. She is a romantic writer, but not a sentimental writer. She cares too fervently about her subject to treat it so. Her books, luminous and introspective, come from, in Yeats's phrase, the "deep heart's core." She reminds us of the simple beauty of daily life, of the extraordinary qualities we find in the people around us, of the resilience of the human spirit, and of the wonder in our own inner strength and potential.

Willa Cather once said of Sarah Orne Jewett, another writer of delicate and sensitive beauty, "To note an artist's limitations is but to define his genius."[17] MacLachlan is a writer with very definite parameters in both style and content. She celebrates the strength of family ties and human relationships, the significance of art and beauty in our lives, the need for human beings to communicate their thoughts and feelings, and the importance of accepting the inevitability of change in our lives. She creates characters possessing great charm, warm humor, and deep sensitivity. And she writes in prose of crystalline purity, with evocative imagery and a structural design as bold and delicately ordered as a Greek temple. Her works represent a passionate embrace of life, a quiet joy in the things of this world, a longing desire for love to prevail.

Notes and References

Chapter One

1. *One Writer's Beginning* (New York: Warner, 1991), 108.
2. Patricia MacLachlan, "Facts and Fictions: On Becoming a Writer," *The Horn Book Magazine* 62 (January/February 1986): 19.
3. Ibid., 20.
4. "MacLachlan," *Something about the Author* 62 (1990): 117–18.
5. MacLachlan, "Facts and Fictions," 19.
6. Patricia MacLachlan, telephone interview by author, 1995.
7. Craig Virden, Delacorte Press, telephone interview by author, 1995.
8. *One Writer's Beginning*, 114.

Chapter Two

1. Charlotte Zolotow and Patricia MacLachlan, "Dialogue between Charlotte Zolotow and Patricia MacLachlan," *The Horn Book Magazine* 65 (November/December 1989): 737.
2. *The Horn Book Magazine* 67 (October/November 1991): 593.
3. E. B. White, *Charlotte's Web* (New York: Harper, 1952), 13. I wish to acknowledge my field editor, Ruth MacDonald, who first noted the similarity of these passages.
4. Jane Yolen, "Patricia MacLachlan," quoted in Gerald J. Senick, ed., *Children's Literature Review* 14 (Detroit: Gale, 1988), 182.
5. Alexandra Johnson, "Meet a Cranky Wizard," *The Christian Science Monitor*, 14 May 1982, B9, quoted in Gerald J. Senick, ed., *Children's Literature Review* 14 (Detroit: Gale, 1988), 182.
6. Jerry Spiegler, "Patricia MacLachlan," quoted in Gerald J. Senick, ed., *Children's Literature Review* 14 (Detroit: Gale, 1988), 182.
7. Zolotow and MacLachlan, "Dialogue," 737.
8. See E. A. Hass, *The New York Times Book Review* 20 (March 1983): 31; and Lizz Timmons, *The School Library Journal* 29.8 (April 1983): 115.

Chapter Three

1. Zolotow and MacLachlan, "Dialogue," 736.

2. MacLachlan, "Facts and Fictions," 22.

3. Ibid., 23.

4. Zena Sutherland, review of *Arthur, for the Very First Time, Bulletin of the Center for Children's Books* 34 (September 1980): 16.

5. Review of *Cassie Binegar, Kirkus Review* 50.17 (1 September 1982): 998.

6. Natalie Babbitt, *Tuck Everlasting* (New York: Farrar, Straus and Giroux, 1975).

7. Roberta Trites, "Claiming the Treasures: Patricia MacLachlan's Organic Postmodernism," *Children's Literature Association Quarterly* 18 (Spring 1993): 25.

8. Ibid., 24.

9. Ibid., 25

Chapter Four

1. MacLachlan, "Facts and Fictions," 24.

2. Patricia MacLachlan, "Painting the Air," *The New Advocate* 3.4 (Fall 1990): 223.

3. Ibid., 225.

4. MacLachlan, interview.

5. Jill Paton Walsh, "History Is Fiction," *The Horn Book Magazine* 48 (January/February 1972): 19.

6. MacLachlan, "Facts and Fictions," 24.

Chapter Five

1. Roberta Seelinger Trites, "Is Flying Extraordinary? Patricia MacLachlan's Use of Aporia," *Children's Literature* 23 (1995): 202.

2. Mary M. Burns, review of *Baby, The Horn Book Magazine* 69 (November/December 1993): 746.

3. MacLachlan, interview.

Chapter Six

1. See particularly the criticism of Roberta Seelinger Trites who focuses on MacLachlan's use of the embedded narrative.

2. Quoted in the preface to Sarah Orne Jewett, *The Country of the Pointed Firs and Other Stories* (Garden City, N.J.: Doubleday, 1956).

3. *Problems of Art: Ten Philosophical Lectures* (New York: Charles Scribner's Sons, 1957), 90.

4. Ibid., 93–94.

5.   Sandra K. Zagarell, "Narrative of Community: The Identification of a Genre," *Sign* 13.3 (1988): 503.

6.   Anne Phillips, " 'Home Itself Put into Song': Music as Metaphorical Community," *The Lion and the Unicorn* 16.2 (December 1992): 145.

7.   Jan Susina, "The Voices of the Prairie: The Use of Music in Laura Ingalls Wilder's *Little House on the Prairie*," *The Lion and the Unicorn* 16.2 (December 1992): 158–66.

8.   *Problems of Art,* 94–95.

9.   Judith Viorst, *Necessary Losses* (New York: Fawcett, 1986), 2.

10.   MacLachlan, interview.

11.   Barbara Hardy, *Tellers and Listeners: The Narrative Imagination* (London: University of London, Athlone Press, 1975), 4.

12.   Betsy Hearne, review of *Sarah, Plain and Tall, Booklist,* 1 May 1985, 1256.

13.   Review of *Tomorrow's Wizard, The Horn Book Magazine,* June 1982, 290.

14.   Review of *Three Names, Publisher's Weekly,* 25 July 1991, 53.

15.   Review of *Baby, Publisher's Weekly,* 16 August 1993, 104.

16.   Virden, interview.

17.   Quoted in the preface to Sarah Orne Jewett, *The Country of the Pointed Firs and Other Stories* (Garden City, N.J.: Doubleday, 1956), 9.

Selected Bibliography

PRIMARY WORKS

Picture Books

All the Places to Love. Illustrated by Mike Wimmer. New York: HarperCollins, 1994.

Mama One, Mama Two. Illustrated by Ruth Lercher Bornstein. New York: Harper & Row, 1982.

Moon, Stars, Frogs, and Friends. Illustrated by Tomie de Paola. New York: Pantheon, 1980.

The Sick Day. Illustrated by William Pene du Bois. New York: Pantheon, 1979.

Three Names. Illustrated by Alexander Pertzoff. New York: HarperCollins, 1991.

Through Grandpa's Eyes. Illustrated by Deborah Ray. New York: Harper & Row, 1980.

What You Know First. Illustrated by Barry Moser. New York: HarperCollins, 1995.

Story Collections

Seven Kisses in a Row. Illustrated by Maria Pia Marrella. New York: Harper & Row, 1983.

Tomorrow's Wizard. Illustrated by Kathy Jacobi. New York: Harper & Row, 1982.

Novels

Arthur, for the Very First Time. Illustrated by Lloyd Bloom. New York: Harper & Row, 1980.

Baby. New York: Delacorte, 1993.

Baby. Screenplay. Turner Broadcasting System, 1996.

Cassie Binegar. New York: Harper & Row, 1982.

The Facts and Fictions of Minna Pratt. New York: Harper & Row, 1988.

Journey. New York: Delacorte, 1991.

Journey. Screenplay. Hallmark Hall of Fame, 1995.

Sarah, Plain and Tall. New York: Harper & Row, 1985.

Sarah, Plain and Tall. Screenplay. Hallmark Hall of Fame, 1990.

Skylark. New York: HarperCollins, 1994.

Skylark. Screenplay. Hallmark Hall of Fame, 1992.
Unclaimed Treasures. New York: Harper & Row, 1984.

Other Writings

"Facts and Fictions: On Becoming a Writer." *The Horn Book Magazine* 62 (January/February 1986): 18–26.
"*Heckedy Peg*." Review of *Heckedy Peg*, by Audrey Wood. *New York Times Book Review*, 8 November 1987, 50.
"*The Mountains of Quilt*." Review of *The Mountains of Quilt*, by Nancy Willard. *New York Times Book Review*, 8 November 1987, 50.
"Painting the Air." *The New Advocate* 3.4 (Fall 1990): 219–25.
"*The Porcelain Cat*." Review of *The Porcelain Cat*, by Michael Patrick Hearn, Diane Dillon, and Leo Dillon. *New York Times Book Review*, 8 November 1987, 50.
With Charlotte Zolotow. "Dialogue between Charlotte Zolotow and Patricia MacLachlan." *The Horn Book Magazine* 65 (November/December 1989): 736–45.

REVIEWS AND CRITICISM

"*All the Places to Love*." (book rev.) *Publishers Weekly*, 21 March 1994, 70.
"*Baby*." (book rev.) *Publishers Weekly*, 16 August 1993, 104.
Bradburn, Frances. "*The Facts and Fictions of Minna Pratt*." (book rev.) *Wilson Library Bulletin* 63 (October 1988): 79.
———. "*Journey*." (book rev.) *Wilson Library Bulletin* 66 (December 1991): 100–101.
———. "*Baby*." (book rev.) *Wilson Library Bulletin* 68 (January 1994): 119–20.
Brown, Rosellen. "*Baby*." (book rev.) *The New York Times Book Review*, 14 November 1993, 34.
Burns, Mary M. "*Three Names*." (book rev.) *The Horn Book Magazine* 67 (November/December 1991): 592–93.
———. "*Baby*." (book rev.) *The Horn Book Magazine* 89 (November/December 1993): 746–47.
Commire, Anne, ed. "Patricia MacLachlan." *Something about the Author* 62. Detroit: Gale Research, 1990, 115–22.
Deveson, Tom. "*Journey*." (book rev.) *Times Educational Supplement*, 14 February 1992, 30.
Elleman, Barbara. "*Unclaimed Treasures*." (book rev.) *Booklist*, July 1984, 1550.
Fader, Ellen. "*Skylark*." (book rev.) *School Library Journal* 40 (March 1994): 222–23.
Fakih, Kimberly Olson. "*The Facts and Fictions of Minna Pratt*." (book rev.) *Publishers Weekly*, 20 May 1988, 92.

Flowers, Ann A. *"Cassie Binegar."* (book rev.) *The Horn Book Magazine* 59 (February 1983): 45–46.

Frederick, Heather Vogel. *"The Facts and Fictions of Minna Pratt."* (book rev.) *New York Times Book Review,* 8 January 1989, 36.

Galda, Lee. *"Three Names."* (book rev.) *The Reading Teacher* 46 (December 1991/January 1992): 330.

Goldberger, Judith. *"Arthur, for the Very First Time."* (book rev.) *Booklist,* 15 October 1980, 328–29.

Hammond, Nancy C. *"Unclaimed Treasures."* (book rev.) *The Horn Book Magazine* 60 (August 1984): 457.

Haviland, Virginia. *"Arthur, for the Very First Time."* (book rev.) *The Horn Book Magazine* 57 (February 1981): 51.

Hearne, Betsy. *"The Sick Day."* (book rev.) *Booklist,* 15 May 1979, 1441.

———. *"Sarah, Plain and Tall."* (book rev.) *Booklist,* 1 May 1985, 1254, 1256.

———. *"Journey."* (book rev.) *The Bulletin of the Center for Children's Books* 45 (October 1991): 44.

Heins, Ethel. *"Sarah, Plain and Tall."* (book rev.) *The Horn Book Magazine* 61 (September/October 1985): 557–58.

Kappelmann, Carol. *"The Facts and Fictions of Minna Pratt."* (book rev.) "The Booktalker": 5. *Wilson Library Bulletin* 64 (September 1989).

Landsberg, Michele. *"Skylark."* (book rev.) *Entertainment Weekly,* 8 April 1994, 69.

Leonard, John. *"Sarah, Plain and Tall."* (television program rev.) *New York,* 4 February 1991, 41–42.

———. *"Skylark."* (television program rev.) *New York,* 8 February 1993, 64.

Marino, Jane. *"Three Names."* (book rev.) *School Library Journal* 37 (July 1991): 60–61.

Martinez, Miriam, and Marcia F. Nash. *"Journey."* (book rev.) *Language Arts* 69 (November 1992): 541.

McDonnell, Christine. *"Through Grandpa's Eyes."* (book rev.) *The Horn Book Magazine* 55 (August 1980): 398.

Negro, Janice Del. *"Skylark."* (book rev.) *Booklist,* 1 January 1994, 827–28.

Noah, Carolyn. *"Journey."* (book rev.) *School Library Journal* 39 (April 1992): 44.

Persson, Lauralyn. *"Baby."* (book rev.) *School Library Journal* 39 (November 1993): 109.

Rochman, Hazel. *"Baby."* (book rev.) *Booklist,* 1 September 1993, 51.

Rockman, Connie C. *"The Facts and Fictions of Minna Pratt."* (book rev.) *School Library Journal* 35 (June/July 1988): 105.

"Sarah, Plain and Tall." (television program rev.) *Variety,* 4 February 1991, 93.

Scott, Tony. *"Skylark."* (television program rev.) *Variety,* 1 February 1993, 101.

Senick, Gerald J., ed. "Patricia MacLachlan." *Children's Literature Review* 14. Detroit: Gale Research, 1988, 177–86.

"Skylark." (book rev.) *Publishers Weekly,* 29 November 1993, 65.

Spangler, William. *"Through Grandpa's Eyes."* (movie rev.) *School Library Journal* 34 (August 1988): 63.

Stewart, Susan. *"Sarah, Plain and Tall."* (sound recording rev.) *Entertainment Weekly,* 28 February 1992, 64–65.

"Three Names." (book rev.) *Publishers Weekly,* 25 July 1991, 53.

"Tomorrow's Wizard." (book rev.) *The Horn Book Magazine* 58 (June 1982): 290.

Trites, Roberta Seelinger. "Claiming the Treasures: Patricia MacLachlan's Organic Postmodernism." *Children's Literature Association Quarterly* 18 (Spring 1993): 23–28.

———. "Nesting: Embedded Narratives as Maternal Discourse in Children's Novels." *Children's Literature Association Quarterly* 18 (Winter 1993–1994): 165–70.

———. "Is Flying Extraordinary? Patricia MacLachlan's Use of Aporia." *Children's Literature* 23. New Haven: Yale University Press, 1995, 202–20.

Tucker, Ken. *"Skylark."* (television program rev.) *Entertainment Weekly,* 5 February 1993, 43.

Vose, Ruth S. *"Journey."* (book rev.) *School Library Journal* 37 (September 1991): 257–58.

Walsh, Jill Paton. "History Is Fiction." *The Horn Book Magazine* 48 (January/February 1972): 17–23.

Watson, Elizabeth S. *"Journey."* (book rev.) *The Horn Book Magazine* 67 (November/December 1991): 737.

Williams, Karen. *"Skylark."* (book rev.) *The Christian Science Monitor,* 6 May 1994, 12.

Zeiger, Hanna B. *"The Facts and Fictions of Minna Pratt."* (book rev.) *The Horn Book Magazine* 64 (July/August 1988): 495–96.

Zwick, Louise Varian, and Mark Zwick. *"Sarah, sencilla y alta."* (book rev.) *School Library Journal* 35 (November 1990): 148.

Index

The Author

David L. Russell holds a Ph.D. in Renaissance literature and is a professor of languages and literature at Ferris State University, where he teaches children's and adolescent literature. In addition to numerous published articles, he has written a textbook, *Literature for Children* (Longman), now in its third edition. He has served on the Board of Directors of the Children's Literature Association and is currently the association's publications chair.

The Editor

Ruth K. MacDonald is college dean for the I Have a Dream Foundation in Hartford, Connecticut. She received her B.A. and M.A. in English from the University of Connecticut, her Ph.D. in English from Rutgers University, and her M.B.A. from the University of Texas at El Paso. She is the author of the volumes on Louisa May Alcott, Beatrix Potter, and Dr. Seuss in Twayne's United States Authors and English Authors series and of the books *Literature for Children in England and America, 1646–1774* (1982) and *Christian's Children: The Influence of John Bunyan's "Pilgrim's Progress" on American Children's Literature* (1989).